KOREAN

HERITAGE

I

HOLLYM
Elizabeth, NJ · SEOUL

First published in 1996
Third printing, 2003
by Hollym International Corp.
18 Donald Place, Elizabeth
New Jersey 07208, U.S.A.
Phone: (908) 353-1655   Fax: (908) 353-0255
http://www.hollym.com

Published simultaneously in Korea
by Hollym Corporation; Publishers
13-13 Gwancheol-dong, Jongno-gu,
Seoul 110-111, Korea
Phone: (02) 735-7551~4   Fax: (02) 730-5149, 8192
http://www.hollym.co.kr e-mail: info@hollym.co.kr

ISBN: 1-56591-077-X
Library of Congress Catalog Card Number: 96-78905

Printed in Korea

Table of Contents

Han-gŭl
The Korean Alphabet

물을 만히 주느니라

이듯고 눈물을 흘리고 벼로장수ᄒᆞ고 그집에저

으니 군시다토아나아가 크게이런디라 신라왕

쥬인이 죽은디라 내엿디 살리오ᄒᆞ고 ᄯᅩ화죽

고적진으로도 라가 빠화죽으니 합졀이롤오디

면엇다 효지라오ᄒᆞ고 칼로합졀의풀을 더버히

진이 롤오디 ᄌᆞ식이아비죽 으믈보고구챠하살

려ᄒᆞᄂᆞ뇨ᄒᆞ고 믈곳잡고 노티아니ᄒᆞ니 거

시니엇디아 비명을 져 ᄇᆞ리고 어믹 ᄌᆞ인 물 ᄉᆞᆺ초

Koreans use their own unique alphabet called *Han-gŭl*. It is considered to be one of the most efficient alphabets in the world and has garnered unanimous praise from language experts for its scientific design and excellence. *Han-gŭl* was created under King Sejong during the Chosŏn Dynasty (1392–1910). In 1446, the first Korean alphabet was proclaimed under the original name *Hunmin chŏng-ŭm*, which literally meant "the correct sounds for the instruction of the people."

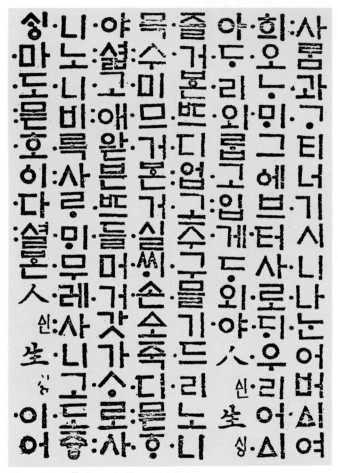

The term *Han-gŭl* refers to the Korean alphabet.
Shown here is *Sŏkpo Sangjŏl* to which the origin of
Han-gŭl can be traced. Early Chosŏn Dynasty.

Han-gŭl

The Korean Alphabet

Koreans use their own unique alphabet called *Han-gŭl*. It is considered to be one of the most efficient alphabets in the world and has garnered unanimous praise from language experts for its scientific design and excellence.

Han-gŭl was invented under King Sejong during the Chosŏn Dynasty (1392-1910). In 1446, the first Korean alphabet was proclaimed under the original name *Hunmin-chŏngŭm*, which literally meant "the correct sounds for the instruction of the people."

King Sejong is considered to be one of the greatest rulers in the history of Korea. Highly respected for his benevolent disposition and diligence, King Sejong was also a passionate scholar whose knowledge and natural talent in all fields of study astounded even the most learned experts.

When he was not performing his official duties, King Sejong enjoyed reading and meditating. He could also be very tenacious at times and would never yield on what he thought was right. Love for the people was the cornerstone of his reign, and he was always ready to

listen to the voices of the common folk. His was a rule of virtue, with the welfare of the people dictating all policy formulations.

King Sejong also established the *Chiphyŏnjŏn*, an academic research institute, inside the palace walls. Noted scholars from all academic disciplines gathered here to engage in lively discussions and also to publish a variety of quality books.

During his reign, King Sejong always deplored the fact that the common people, ignorant of the complicated Chinese characters that were being used by the educated, were not able to read and write. He understood their frustration in not being able to read or to communicate their thoughts and feelings in written words.

The Chinese script was used by the intelligentsia of the country, but being of foreign origin, it could not fully express the words and meaning of Korean thoughts and spoken language. Therefore, common people with legitimate complaints had no way of submitting their grievances to the appropriate authorities, other than through oral communication,

Hunmin-chŏngŭm haerye uses five explanations and one example to explain Han-gŭl (right)

Han-gŭl was created under King Sejong and was first proclaimed as *Hunmin-chŏngŭm*.

and they had no way to record for posterity the agricultural wisdom and knowledge they had gained through years of experience.

King Sejong felt great sympathy for the people. As a revolutionary ruler strongly dedicated to national identity and cultural independence, he immediately searched for solutions. What he envisioned was a set of letters that was uniquely Korean and easily learnable, rendering it accessible and usable for the common people.

Thus, the *Hunmin-chŏngŭm* was born. In the preface of its proclamation, King Sejong states as follows:

"Being of foreign origin, Chinese characters are incapable of capturing uniquely Korean meanings. Therefore, many common people have no way to express their thoughts and feelings. Out of my sympathy for their difficulties, I have invented a set of 28 letters. The letters are very easy to learn, and it is my fervent hope that they improve the quality of life of all people." The statement captures the essence of King Sejong's determination and dedication to cultural independence and commitment to the welfare of the people.

When first proclaimed by King Sejong, *Hunmin-chŏngŭm* had 28 letters in all, of which only 24 are in use today. The 24 letters are as

follows.

Consonants: ㄱ (k), ㄴ (n), ㄷ (t), ㄹ (r or l), ㅁ (m), ㅂ (p), ㅅ (s or sh), ㅇ (voiceless), ㅈ (ch), ㅊ (ch'), ㅋ (k'), ㅌ (t'), ㅍ (p'), ㅎ (h)

Vowels: ㅏ (a), ㅑ (ya), ㅓ (ŏ), ㅕ (yŏ), ㅗ (o), ㅛ (yo), ㅜ (u), ㅠ (yu), ㅡ (ŭ), ㅣ (i)

The basic letters of the alphabet when *Hunmin-chŏngŭm* was first created numbered eight; they were the consonants " ㄱ, ㄴ, ㅁ, ㅅ, ㅇ " and the vowels " •, ㅡ, ㅣ "

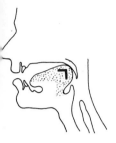

Root of the letter " ㄱ"(k). Back of the tongue sticks near the uvula.

The reason consonants and vowels were separated was due to their differing functions when two letters were combined to form a syllable. *Hunmin-chŏngŭm* is basically a form of hieroglyph. Consonants, the initial sound letters, resemble a person's speech organs. The shape of each letter is based on the form of different sound articulation units. Other consonants, excluding by adding additional strokes to the basic forms, based on the strength of the sounds.

" ㄱ (kiyŏk)": To pronounce this letter, part of the tongue touches the molar teeth and sticks near the uvula. The shape of the letter is based on the lateral form of this process.

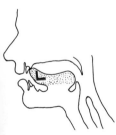

Root of the letter " ㄴ"(n). The tip of the tongue sticks to the upper gums.

" ㄴ (niŭn)": To pronounce this letter, the front of the tongue curves and the tip of the tongue sticks to the upper gums. The shape of the letter is based on the lateral form of this process.

A portrait of King Sejong, creator of Korea's own alphabet, *Hunmin-chŏngŭm* (left).

" ㅁ (miŭm)": To pronounce this letter, the upper and lower lips are joined. The shape of the letter is based on the form of the joined lips.

"ㅅ(shiot)": To pronounce this letter, the tip of the tongue and the upper teeth are brought close together, and sound is created by blowing through the narrowed passage. The shape of the letter is based on the form of the teeth during the process.

"ㅇ(iŭng)": To pronounce this letter that is created by stimulating the uvula, the throat assumes a round shape, hence the form of the consonant.

Nine additional letters were made by adding strokes to the five basic consonants based on the strength of the sounds, as follows.

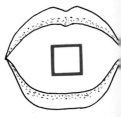

Root of the letter "ㅁ" (m). Joined lips.

ㄱ - ㅋ

ㄴ - ㄷ, ㅌ

ㅁ - ㅂ, ㅍ

ㅅ - ㅈ, ㅊ

ㅇ - ㆆ, ㅎ

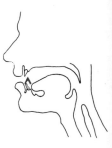

Root of the letter "ㅅ" (s). Sharp teeth.

However, "ㆆ" is no longer used. The vowels, on the other hand, were created in the image of the sky, land, and man. That is '·' resembles the roundness of the sky, '—' represents the flat land and 'ㅣ' is the image of a standing man. The other vowels "ㅏ, ㅑ, ㅓ, ㅕ, ㅗ, ㅛ, ㅜ, ㅠ" are variations of these three basic vowels.

The creation of the *Hunmin-chŏngŭm* was truly a remarkable accomplishment. Creating consonants based on a person's speech organs and vowels based on the shapes of the sky, land, and man was truly a revolutionary and unprecedented process.

King Sejong and the scholars of the *Chiphyŏnjŏn*, inventors of the Korean alphabet, considered human

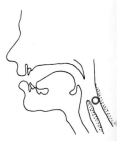

Root of the letter "ㅇ" (voiceless). round-shaped throat.

sounds as being more than mere physical phenomena. They assumed that an invisible yet more powerful principle was the controlling force behind these phenomena. They adhered to the principle that human sounds and all universal phenomena are all based on *yin-yang* (positive-negative) and *ohaeng* (the five primary elements: metal, wood, water, fire and earth). Hence, they thought it natural that there be a common link between sounds and the changing of the seasons

Yŏngpi (right) and a rubbed copy (left). This is the oldest stone monument written in *Han-gŭl* and was used when *Hunmin-chŏngŭm* was created.

and between sounds and music.

A Korean syllable is divided into three parts: *ch'o-sŏng* (initial consonant), *chungsŏng* (peak vowel), and *chongsŏng* (final consonant). This is the basic framework that King Sejong and the *Chiphyŏnjŏn* scholars adhered to when creating the letters. *Chong-sŏng* was not separately created and was a repetition of the *ch'o-sŏng*. Therefore, *Han-gŭl* is capable of creating thousands of words by combining the consonants and vowels.

A work of fiction written in *Han-gŭl*, *The Story of Hong Kil-tong*. The Korean alphabet.

The Korean alphabet.

Vowels / Consonants	ㅏ [a]	ㅑ [ya]	ㅓ [ŏ]	ㅕ [yŏ]	ㅗ [o]	ㅛ [yo]	ㅜ [u]	ㅠ [yu]	ㅡ [ŭ]	ㅣ [i]
ㄱ [k, g]	가	갸	거	겨	고	교	구	규	그	기
ㄴ [n]	나	냐	너	녀	노	뇨	누	뉴	느	니
ㄷ [t, d]	다	댜	더	뎌	도	됴	두	듀	드	디
ㄹ [r, l]	라	랴	러	려	로	료	루	류	르	리
ㅁ [m]	마	먀	머	며	모	묘	무	뮤	므	미
ㅂ [p, b]	바	뱌	버	벼	보	뵤	부	뷰	브	비
ㅅ [s, sh]	사	샤	서	셔	소	쇼	수	슈	스	시
ㅇ [衆]	아	야	어	여	오	요	우	유	으	이
ㅈ [ch, j]	자	쟈	저	져	조	죠	주	쥬	즈	지
ㅊ [ch']	차	챠	처	쳐	초	쵸	추	츄	츠	치
ㅋ [k']	카	캬	커	켜	코	쿄	쿠	큐	크	키
ㅌ [t']	타	탸	터	텨	토	툐	투	튜	트	티
ㅍ [p']	파	퍄	퍼	펴	포	표	푸	퓨	프	피
ㅎ [h]	하	햐	허	혀	호	효	후	휴	흐	히

First copy of Korea's first privately-owned newspaper, the *Tongnip Shinmun* (The Independent). Launched on April 7, 1896, the paper was the country's first to use only *Han-gŭl*.

ㄱ+ㅏ=가 (ka)	ㄴ+ㅏ=나 (na)	ㄷ+ㅏ=다 (da)	ㄹ+ㅏ=라 (ra)
ㄱ+ㅑ=갸 (kya)	ㄴ+ㅑ=냐 (nya)	ㄷ+ㅑ=댜 (dya)	ㄹ+ㅑ=랴 (rya)
ㄱ+ㅓ=거 (kŏ)	ㄴ+ㅓ=너 (nŏ)	ㄷ+ㅓ=더 (dŏ)	ㄹ+ㅓ=러 (rŏ)
ㄱ+ㅕ=겨 (kyŏ)	ㄴ+ㅕ=녀 (nyŏ)	ㄷ+ㅕ=뎌 (dyŏ)	ㄹ+ㅕ=려 (ryŏ)
ㄱ+ㅗ=고 (ko)	ㄴ+ㅗ=노 (no)	ㄷ+ㅗ=도 (do)	ㄹ+ㅗ=로 (ro)
ㄱ+ㅛ=교 (kyo)	ㄴ+ㅛ=뇨 (nyo)	ㄷ+ㅛ=됴 (dyo)	ㄹ+ㅛ=료 (ryo)
ㄱ+ㅜ=구 (ku)	ㄴ+ㅜ=누 (nu)	ㄷ+ㅜ=두 (du)	ㄹ+ㅜ=루 (ru)
ㄱ+ㅠ=규 (kyu)	ㄴ+ㅠ=뉴 (nyu)	ㄷ+ㅠ=듀 (dyu)	ㄹ+ㅠ=류 (ryu)
ㄱ+ㅡ=그 (kŭ)	ㄴ+ㅡ=느 (nŭ)	ㄷ+ㅡ=드 (dŭ)	ㄹ+ㅡ=르 (rŭ)
ㄱ+ㅣ=기 (ki)	ㄴ+ㅣ=니 (ni)	ㄷ+ㅣ=디 (di)	ㄹ+ㅣ=리 (ri)

As the above examples clearly show, *Han-gŭl*, with only 14 consonants and 10 vowels, is capable of expressing virtually any sound.

The Korean language has a well-developed and expansive vocabulary, and therefore, it is very difficult to express fully in foreign letter. However, due to its scientific design, it is quite easy to approximate the sounds of foreign words in the Korean alphabet. Following are some examples of English words expressed in *Han-gŭl*.

London	New York	Hong Kong
런던	뉴욕	홍콩

I	am	a	boy	Good morning
아이	엠	어	보이	굿모닝

In particular, because of its simplicity and the rather small number of letters, *Han-gŭl* is very easy to learn even by children and foreigners.

It is no coincidence that by the time they reach the ages of two or three, most Korean children are already capable of expressing their feelings and thoughts, albeit in primitive form. By the time they reach school age, most exhibit mastery of *Han-gŭl*, which is indeed a rare phenomena throughout the world. This fact clearly attests to the easy learnability and accessibility of the Korean alphabet.

It is ironic that the strongest proof of the easy learnability of the alphabet came from the critics who argued against the creation of *Hunmin-chŏngŭm*. Some scholars vehemently voiced their views against the "new" alphabet because of its easy learnability, and in derision, they called it *Ach'imgŭl* (morning letters) or *Amk'ŭl* (women's letters).

Ach'imgŭl meant that it could be learned in one morning. For those scholars who had spent years on learning the complicated letters of the Chinese language, *Han-gŭl* did not appear to be worthy of learning. *Amk'ŭl* meant that even women who had no academic training or background could easily learn the new alphabet. Back then there were those who

With a large number of programs written in *Han-gŭl*, people can incorporate computers into their lives without difficulty.

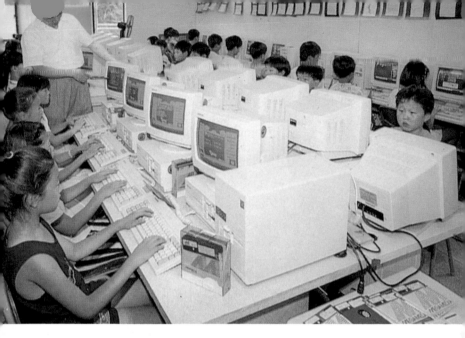

considered the pursuit of academic studies and the subject of reading and writing to be the sole domain of a few privileged scholars.

Such misconceptions were the result of confusing simple linguistic learning with more advanced academic studies. Without learning the basic alphabet, reading and writing would be impossible, let alone the study of more advanced subjects. Without being able to read and write, there can be no indirect communication of one's feelings and thoughts. Surely, King Sejong's intent was to enrich the lives of the people by introducing *Han-gŭl*, and not to make scholars out of all his subjects.

Throughout history, *Han-gŭl* has been at the root of the Korean culture, helping to preserve its national identity and independence.

Illiteracy is virtually nonexistent in Korea. This is another fact that attests to the easy learnability of *Han-gŭl*. It is not uncommon for a foreigner to gain a working knowledge of *Han-gŭl* after one or two hours of intensive studying. In addition, because of its scientific design, *Han-gŭl* lends itself to easy mechanization. In this age of computers, many people now are able to incorporate computers into their lives without difficulties, thanks to a large number of programs written in *Han-gŭl*.

Because *Han-gŭl* is simple and easy to learn, illiteracy is virtually nonexistent in Korea. *Han-gŭl* calligraphy is an art.

When first proclaimed under the name of Hunmin chong-ŭm, Han-gŭl had 28 letters in all, of which only 24 are in use today. Those are as follows;

Consonants: ㄱ ㄴ ㄷ ㄹ ㅁ ㅂ ㅅ ㅇ ㅈ ㅊ ㅋ ㅌ ㅍ ㅎ

Vowels: ㅏ ㅑ ㅓ ㅕ ㅗ ㅛ ㅜ ㅠ ㅡ ㅣ

Printing Heritage

In the cultural history of the world, the Korean people stand out as having created a brilliant tradition in printing. Wood-block printing began in the 8th century in Korea. The world's first metal typeface was developed by the Koreans more than 200 years before Gutenberg in Germany.

Printing Heritage

In the cultural history of the world, the Korean people stand out as having created a brilliant tradition in printing. Wood-block printing began in the 8th century in Korea. The world's first metal typeface was developed by the Koreans more than 200 years before Gutenberg in Germany.

Long before the use of letters, human beings have used various symbols and signs to communicate and to keep track of records. The engraved symbols and pictures on the surface of stones used by the primitive ancestors of Koreans can be seen in the stone carvings discovered in Ch'ŏnjŏn-ri, Ulchu. After letters were introduced, transcription greatly enhanced the effectiveness of indirect communication. Engraved in stone or metal, the symbols and letters could withstand the erosion of thousands of years, and rubbings could be taken from them for the education of future generations.

Korea's printing tradition is the oldest in the world. The *Taejanggyŏng* (Tripitaka Koreana) which was carved from 1236 to 1251 is preserved in Changgyŏnggak Hall at Haeinsa Temple.

After Buddhism was introduced to Korea in 372 A.D. during the Three Kingdoms period, transcription and engraving in stone or metal became a wide-spread practice to propagate the teachings in Buddhist scriptures. The missionary zeal of the believers led to an enormous increase in the production of paper and ink-sticks.Thus, as early as the Three Kingdoms period, Koreans were transferring their knowledge in making paper and ink-sticks to Japan. They were also exporting their products to China, where the paper later came to be well known as "Shilla" paper, "Koryŏ" paper, or "Chosŏn" paper, depending on the different periods in Korea. In short, with the religious fervor of Buddhism providing the impetus, the necessary ingredients for the early development of printing—paper, ink, and the message—were well in place during

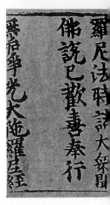

The world's oldest existing wood blocks were used to print *Mugujŏnggwang-taedaranigyŏng* (Pure Light Dharani Sutra).

This metal-block of a sutra (Buddhist scripture), produced sometime between the late Unified Shilla period and the early Koryŏ period, well illustrates the technique in carving blocks that served both as a base for making a rubbed copy and as a prototype for wood-block printing.

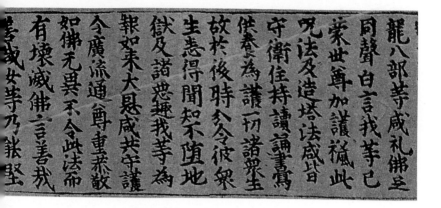

the Three Kingdoms period.

Historical records indicate that wood-block printing was being practiced in Korea in the beginning of the 8th century. A Buddhist scripture printed from wood-blocks dating to the Shilla period, was retrieved from Pulguksa temple in Kyŏngju. The title of the scripture is *Mugujŏnggwang-taedaranigyŏng* (Pure Light Dharani Sutra). It is presumed to have been translated into Chinese characters by a monk named Mit'asan around the year 704. One record also indicates that it was placed within the stone pagoda of Hwangboksa temple in 706. Others place it as the scripture that inspired the construction of numerous pagodas in Japan. Since the pagoda at Pulguksa temple from where the scripture was retrieved was built in 751, the scripture itself must have been printed well before that year. Though it is small, the print reveals the characteristics of early wood-block printing in Korea, and attests to the lofty heights in cultural accomplishments that the Korean people at the time reached. It remains the world's oldest remaining printed material.

Meanwhile, Ch'oe Ch'i-wŏn, the great scholar of the Shilla Kingdom, wrote in one of his many books that a collection of Shilla poetry had been printed and sent to an envoy of T'ang in China. The statement is testimony to the widespread use of printing during the Shilla period.

Printing further developed during the Koryŏ Dynasty (918 - 1392). Having adopted Buddhism as the state religion, numerous Buddhist temples were built, and printing was promoted for Buddhist teachings during the Koryŏ Dynasty. Of them, the oldest remaining text is *Pohyŏpindaranigyŏng*, printed at Ch'ongjisa temple in 1007. It shows the highly refined craftsmanship of Koryŏ wood-block printers.

During the reign of Hyŏnjong (1010-1031), the printing blocks for *Ch'ojo Taejanggyŏng* (first trimmed Tripitaka) were carved (1011-1031). Later the blocks for *Sokchang*, a comprehensive collection of the studies and footnotes on the Tripitaka were also made (1091-1101). The blocks for both works were burned to ashes during the Mongol invasion in 1232. The King ordered them re-made, even under the hardships of war, which took place between 1237 and 1248. The resulting masterpieces have been preserved to this day at Haeinsa temple in Hapch'ŏn-gun county, Kyŏng-sangnam-do province and are the world's oldest remaining wood-blocks for the Tripitaka. They are also the most accurate and comprehensive, used by the Chinese and Japanese as the standard reference in Buddhism studies. Printing flourished in other temples

A wood block for the Tripitaka Koreana housed at Haeinsa Temple.

皇帝曰金石刻盡始皇帝所為也今襲號而金石刻辭不稱始皇帝其於久遠也如後嗣為之者不稱成功盛德丞相臣斯臣去疾御史大夫臣德昧死言臣請具刻詔書金石刻因明白矣臣昧死請制曰可

during the Koryŏ Dynasty as well, churning out Buddhist scriptures, collections of poetry and essays by monks. Confucian teachings, medical treatises, historical writings, poetry and essays by noted scholars were also carved in wood for printing.

In the *Tongguk-isangguk-chip* (Collected Works of Minister Yi of Koryŏ), the author notes that printing with metal type was already being done in the Koryŏ Kingdom (918-1392).

Koryŏ Dynasty printing is noted for its invention of metal typeface. With wood-blocks alone, the exploding demand for quality printed materials could not be fully met. The clever people of the Koryŏ period overcame this challenge by inventing characters cast in metal. The exact date of the invention is difficult to identify. Some argue that it was during the 11th century; others say it was sometime during the 12th. One author writing on wood blocks in 1239 indicated that metal characters were around well before 1232. Furthermore, the famous scholar-official Yi Kyu-bo (1168-1241) wrote in his masterpiece *Tongguk-isangguk-chip* (Collected Works of Minister Yi of Korea) that 28 copies of *Sangjŏng-yemun* (prescribed ritual texts) were printed with metal characters.

One of Koryŏ's early metallograph works, *Paegun*

hwasang ch'orok Pulcho chikchi shimch'e yojŏl (the Selected Sermons of Buddhist Sages and Sŏn Masters) printed at Hŭngdŏksa temple in Ch'ŏngju in 1377, is kept at the French National Library in Paris. The book, which was printed at a local temple, is proof that metal type was widely used during Koryŏ. In the book Koryŏsa

Pulcho chikchi shimch'e yojŏl (The Selected Sermons of Buddhist Sages and Sŏn Masters) was printed with metal type during the Koryŏ Dynasty.

(History of Koryŏ), it is recorded that in 1392 King Kongyang gave the government office *Sŏjŏkwŏn* (books and publications center) the responsibility of overseeing all matters related to casting metal types and printing books.

During the Chosŏn Dynasty (1392-1910), metal, wood, and even ceramic characters were used for printing. Metal types were also called *Chuja* (cast characters) and were made of copper, zinc, iron, and other metals. The founder of the Chosŏn Dynasty, King T'aejo kept alive the operations of Koryŏ's *Sŏjŏk-wŏn*. During the time of King T'aejong, a separate casting office –*Chujaso* or type casting center– was established (1403). The printed materials consisted largely of books

Koreans are studying their printing heritage by recreating the characters used in the *Pulcho chikchi shimch'e yojŏl*.

Kyemi-ja, first metal characters made in the Chosŏn Dynasty (1403) (left).
Kyŏngja-ja was made by complementing defects of *Kyemi-ja* (1420) (right).

and documents deemed necessary by the government. They were distributed to the central and local administration, village schools, scholars and officials. For further distribution, wood- block printing was employed, as copies from metal types were limited.

The first set of metal characters made by the *Chujaso* during the Chosŏn Dynasty was the *Kyemi-ja* characters, named after the year (1403) in which it came out. In 1420, it was refined into the *Kyŏngja-ja* characters. The third set, the *Kabin-ja* characters came out in 1434, King Sejong mobilized the efforts of the scholars and engineers of astronomical implements employed at his court to create the set. The result was a set far more exquisite than the previous ones, and it could print twice as many copies as the *Kyŏngja-ja* set. The great King also had his scholars and craftsmen develop printing characters for *Han-gŭl*, the Korean alphabet. The beauty and harmony of the printed Chinese and Korean characters attest to the preeminence of the *Kabin-ja* among all metal characters that were developed in Korea. Thus, the Chosŏn court had the set reproduced six times. In 1436, it produced the *Pyŏngjin-ja*, named after the year. They were the first soldered characters in the world.

Afterward, numerous other character sets were developed based on various styles of writing; however, most were destroyed or plundered during the *Imjin Waeran* (Japanese invasions of 1592-1598). When they retreated, the invaders took with them countless ceramic artisans and type-casting craftsmen, who later became the seeds for the flowering of printing in Japan.

Kabin-ja, one of the best Korean metal characters. Produced in 1434 (left).
Pyŏngja-ja made in 1516 (right).

Amid the destruction of the war, it was difficult to secure the raw materials needed to make printing characters. But even then, the soldiers of *Hullyŏn togam* (military training command of Chosŏn) printed books using wooden characters and sold them to raise money for the war efforts. The characters were known as the *Hullyŏn togam-ja*, and they were used until the efforts resumed to make metal characters.

Kwanghae-gun, the 15th king of Chosŏn, rebuilt the casting office and renamed it *Chuja togam*, and had it create the *Muo-ja* characters in 1618. That was followed by the *Hyŏnjong shillok-ja* characters, intended specifically to print the history of King Hyŏnjong's reign, as well as a number of other character sets. Altogether, during the Chosŏn period, some 40 metal character sets were

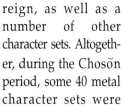

There were virtually no mistakes in the ancient books printed in Korea.
This is a copy of *Sŏksshiwonryu*, a Buddhist text, and the wood block used to print it.

created by the central government offices. Their names typically indicated the year in which they were made, the agency that made them and the individual who provided the prototype character forms.

Needless to say, local administrations, temples, villages and schoolhouses were also active in printing. In the local regions, wooden characters or blocks were largely employed.

Metal typography and printing flourished during the Choson Dynasty, but the technique of wood-block printing inherited from Koryo also continued. In early Choson, Buddhism among the royalty, persevered even in spite of the official anti-Buddhism policy of the new dynasty, provided the support for the continued printing of Buddhist scriptures. During King Sejo's time, *Kan-gyong togam*, a special printing office was established to translate and print Buddhist works. The influence of the royal court could be seen in the delicate engraving on the printing blocks.

But the largest portion of wood-block printing during the Choson period took place at the local government offices, temples, and village schoolhouses. Equipped with the necessary manpower and material resources, temples were particularly active in producing Buddhist scriptures as well as poetry and essay collections and even Confucian writings. They were the professional wood-block printers of the time.

Wood-block printing remained quite popular throughout the Choson Dynasty, as there was no limit to the number of copies that could be made and the blocks were easy to keep. But as the centuries passed

直指心経字
Chikchi shimkyŏng-ja

癸未字
Kyemi-ja

Various metal types used in Korea from the Koryŏ to the Choson period.

庚子字

Kŏngja-ja

by, the quality declined, and the engraving became coarse.

It is noteworthy that misprints are hardly ever found in Korea's printing heritage. This, however, is not surprising, since the system did not permit error. As indicated in *Kyŏngguk taejŏn* (Grand Code of Managing the Nation) and other historical records, punishment of related workers was severe: for a single error found in an entire volume, everyone, from the top supervisor to the lowest level intern, was caned thirty times; five or more mistakes led to dismissal.

Indeed, the Chosŏn Dynasty developed a uniquely rich tradition in printing: for five centuries, the government took the lead in creating metal characters, local entities kept alive the tradition of wood-block printing, and great books of impeccable type were printed. Throughout world history, it is difficult to find a comparable example.

However, these days, Korea is an importer as far as printing and publications are concerned, despite the honor of having been the world's first user of metal type. There is a growing awareness that the glory of the past should be revived.

甲寅字

Kabin-ja

With the religious fervor of
Buddhism, transcription and
engraving in stone or metal
became a wide-spread practice.
So, you can say Korea owes many
part of printing tradition to
Buddhism.

Folk Paintings

Folk painting comprises the so-called "functional" pictures widely used by commoners in old Korea to decorate their homes or to express their wishes for a long, happy life. Folk paintings, normally unsigned, often depict the same motifs as those of the so-called "orthodox" paintings including landscapes, flowers and birds, but abound with humor and simple and naive ideas about life and the world.

Folk Paintings

Folk painting comprises the so-called "functional" pictures widely used by commoners in old Korea to decorate their home or to express their wishes for a long, happy life. Folk paintings, normally unsigned, often depict the same motifs as those of the so-called "orthodox" paintings including landscapes, flowers and birds, but abound with humor and simple and naive ideas about life and the world.

Ancient Korean folk paintings present the age-old customs of the Korean nation. Their repeated themes well represent the unique lifestyle of the Korean people, their dreams, wishes and artistic imagination. Though folk painting, typified by simple compositions of stylized motifs and bright primary colors, is usually considered a low form of art, it does not necessarily mean that all paintings in this genre are technically inferior to those categorized as standard painting.

Folk painting actually includes a wide variety of paintings ranging from those by high-caliber

In ancient Korean folk paintings are portrayed the age-old customs of the Korean nation. A folk painting showing a Korean traditional wedding.

professional painters at the royal court to those by wandering monks and unknown amateur artists. Some pieces demonstrate marvelous artistry, but some are considerably less skilled and sophisticated. The earliest examples of Korean folk painting, or *minhwa*, date from prehistoric times.

Picture and patterns in folk style are found in artifacts from all periods, including Neolithic rock carvings, early bronze articles, the murals and bricks in the tombs of the Koguryŏ period (37 B.C-A.D.668), and handicraft objects from the Koryŏ (918-1392)and the Chosŏn period (1392-1910). It may be said that folk painting has its roots in animal patterns on the primitive rock carvings, the four Taoist guardians and immortals in the tomb murals, pictures of the ten longevity symbols, hunting scenes and bricks ornamented with landscape designs.

Folk paintings were produced by artists who obviously belonged to a low social class in traditional Korea. But their paintings were used by people of all social strata, from the royal household and temples down to the farmers in remote villages. The paintings were needed for rites in various religious

The origins of Korean folk painting can also be found in the murals of Koguryŏ (right).

denominations like shamanism, Taoism, Buddhism and Confucianism, and for decoration of public facilities and private homes. They were intended mainly to stand for the common wishes of the public to repel evil sprits and to invoke good fortune, or to depict daily customs and moral concepts.

Consequently, folk paintings may be divided largely into two categories: religious paintings and nonreligious paintings. Religious paintings depict shamanist, Taoist and Buddhist themes as well as Confucian precepts for ancestor worship and moral discipline. Non-religious paintings include genre pictures, portaits, illustrations of ancient episodes, documentary pictures, maps and astronomical charts. Folk paintings may be classified into the following

categories by theme:

1. Tao-shamanist paintings

Longevity symbols : Pictures of the ten longevity symbols figure most prominently among folk paintings of this category. The ten longevity symbols, including the sun, clouds, rock, water, bamboo, pine, crane, deer, turtle and the fungus of immortality, are often presented all together in a single picture. Also representing the predominant wishes for a long life are pictures of pine and crane, cranes or deer in large groups, and cranes and peaches presented with sea waves. It is of special note that the royal throne had a picture of the sun and the moon rising over a mountain of five peaks as a favorite backdrop.

Directional guardians and the 12 zodiacal symbols:

Ancient folk paintings often depict the five directional spirits and the animal gods symbolizing the 12 zodiacal signs as an expression of the desire to disperse evil spirits and invoke happiness. The five directional spirits are the blue dragon of the west, the white tiger of the east, the red peacock of the south, the black turtle-snake of the north and the yellow emperor of the center. As time passed, the red peacock was substitued with a phoenix or a mythical animal called the kirin, and the black turtle-snake with a turtle. The 12 zodiacal signs are represented by the mouse, ox, tiger, rabbit, dragon, snake, horse, sheep, monkey, rooster, dog and pig.

The royal throne had a picture of the sun and the moon rising over a mountain of five peaks as a backdrop, symbolizing longevity.

Tiger : The tiger was among the most popular motif in Korean folk painting. Originating probably from the mythical "white tiger" as the guardian spirits of the east, the tiger was often personified in Korean folklore. A notable characteristic about the tiger as featured in Korean folk traditions is seldom portrayed as a ferocious beast but as a friendly animal, sometimes even funny and stupid. The tiger appears as a docile companion and messenger of the mountain spirit in

Immortals have been important motifs in the Korean folk tradition. Painting of immortals enjoying a game of go.

Magpie and tiger. The tiger was one of the favorite motifs in Korean folk painting (right).

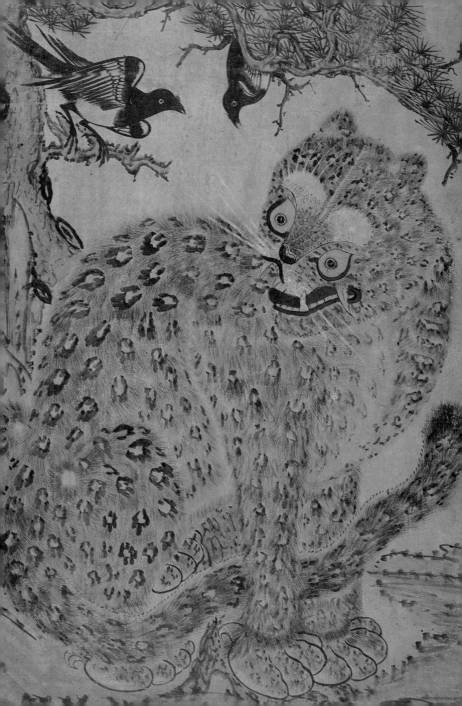

many folk paintings. It often appears with a magpie on a pine tree, a rooster or a lion. The magpie in Korean folkore is an auspicious bird believed to bring good news.

Immortals : As symbols of the Taoist ideal of harmony with nature as a way to achieve an eternal life, immortals have been important motifs in the Korean folk tradition over the centuries. Immortals, often portrayed as hermits in the mountains, were also believed to help the mortals to live happily, content with good health, wealth and many children.

The mountain spirit and dragon king : The popular mountain spirit and the dragon king motifs have their origins in two famous figures in Korean history,Tan-gun and Munmu. Tan-gun is the progenitor of the Korean people who is said to have turned into a mountain spirit in old age; King Munmu of the Shilla Kingdom is said to have become the dragon king after death, and his remains were buried in the East Sea in accordance with his will. The mountain spirit is portrayed in folk paintings as a benevolent old man with a white beard, accompanied by a tiger messenger. The dragon king is usually depicted as a mighty animal flying amidst the clouds over the sea of high waves. The pictures of the mountain spirit and the dragon king motifs are housed at shrines in the mountains or by the sea as the guardians of peace and prosperity of the nation. Also appearing frequently in ancient folk paintings are various other Taoist and shamanistic deities as well as famous kings, generals, ministers and their wives.

A folk painting with various animals believed to bring good luck.

2.Buddhist paintings

Buddhist temples and hermitages across the country are rich archives of folk paintings, ranging from large icon images for ritual use to illustrations for sutras and anecdotes about famous monks and their portraits. These temple paintings are noted for simple compositions and bright colors.

3. Confucian paintings

Confucianism, based on the teachings of Confucius and other sages, has developed in Korea as an important intellectual and moral belief system. It also incorporated the nation's unique shaman and Taoist concepts of ancestor worship and respect of nature.

A painting depicting the desire to enjoy long life with good health, affluence, and high social position.

Folk paintings in this category, including character designs of the popular themes of loyalty and filial piety, pictures depicting the life stories of renowned scholars, and a carp jumping up from the river to transform into a dragon, symbolizing the widespread aspiration for distinguished academic achievement and a successful careers in officialdom.

4. Decorative paintings

A great majority of ancient folk paintings handed down to the present were used for decorative purposes. These paintings generally repeat popular motifs with relatively poor techniques, but attest to the nation's religious tradition harmonizing various faiths

This character design can be classified as Confucian painting (left).

such as shamanism, Taoism, Buddhism and Confucianism. Ancient Korean folk paintings have the following characteristics: First, the folk paintings show an unequivocal yearning for happiness. They stand for the universal desire to chase away evil spirits and to enjoy a long life blessed with good health, materialistic affluence and high social position.

Second, folk paintings attest to the honesty and simpilcity of the Korean people. The paintings are unrefined, sometimes even childish and crude. Yet they demomstrate the nature of the Korean people, prone to simplicity and unpretentiousness.

Third, the folk painting show the deep love of Korean for nature, humankind and the deities. They are full of humanity, peace and warmth of the heart, which can seldom be found in orthodox paintings.

Fourth, the folk paintings, with their bold compositions, dynamic brushwork and intense colors, display the indomitable will and courage of an agrarian society, oppression from the class and foreign invasions.

Fifth, the folk paintings abound with humor and satire. They manifest the considerable mental strength of the Korean people who are able to wisely surmount difficulties. Pains and sorrows are sublimated into joys and happiness with rich humor and satire.

Sixth, Korean folk paintings have their unique style which was derived from the indigenous artistic flair of the Korean people.

Korean folk paintings show an unequivocal yearning for happiness.
This picture is based on the ten longevity symbols.

A great majority of ancient folk painting handed down to the present were used for decorative purposes. These paintings generally repeat popular motifs with relatively poor techniques, but attest to the nations' religious tradition harmonizing various faiths.

Tanch'ŏng

he use of *tanch'ŏng* in Korea dates back many centuries, and the skillful
chniques developed long ago are still preserved today. *Tanch'ŏng* refers to a
orean-style decorative coloring used in buildings or equipment to present beauty
d majesty, and is done by applying various patterns and paintings in certain areas.
ve basic colors are used: red, blue, yellow, black and white.

Tanch'ŏng

The use of *tanch'ŏng* in Korea dates back many centuries, and the skillful techniques developed long ago are still preserved today. *Tanch'ŏng* refers to a Korean-style decorative coloring used in buildings or equipment to present beauty and majesty, and is done by applying various patterns and paintings in certain areas. Five basic colors are used: red, blue, yellow, black and white.

In addition to its decorative function, *tanch'ŏng* was done for practical reasons as well. It was used to prolong the life of the building or equipment and conceal the crudeness of the quality of the material used, while emphasizing the characteristics and the grade or ranks that the building or object possessed. *Tanch'ŏng* also provided conformity and diversity.

Ordinarily *tanch'ŏng* refers to the painting of buildings constructed of wood. Coloring of other buildings or objects may be found as well, however, adding majesty to a stone building, structural statues or artifacts.

Tanch'ŏng is a highly developed art in Korea. *Tanch'ŏng* of Hwaŏmsa Temple in Kurye, Chŏllanam-do province.

Due to the absence of buildings from ancient times, the history of Korean *tanch'ŏng* can only be traced via murals in old tombs during the Three Kingdoms period (57 B.C.-A.D. 668). Particularly in murals of old tombs from the Koguryŏ Kingdom (37 B.C.-A.D. 668), there remain diverse colored patterns which show the appearance of *tanch'ŏng* and architectural characteristics of that period. Along with these murals, colored pictures and lacquerwork excavated from tombs also show the elements of *tanch'ŏng*.

According to the historical records of the Three Kingdoms, only nobility with the rank of *sŏnggol* (those in the royal family qualified to be king) could use the five colors during the Ancient Shilla Kingdom (57 B.C.-A.D. 668). Unfortunately, no building decorated with *tanch'ŏng* from that era remains today. Only through evidence from architectural remains excavated in Kyŏngju, the capital of the Shilla Kingdom, can it be deduced that *tanch'ŏng* during that period was quite delicate and beautiful.

In the *Sŏnhwapongsa Koryŏ-Togyŏng* (Illustrated Account of Koryo), written in the 12th century by the Chinese scholar Sŏgung, it is noted that Koryŏ people enjoyed building royal palaces. According to the text, the structure of the places where the king stayed was constructed with round pillars and a square headpiece. The ridge of the roof was colorfully decorated and its configurational structure appeared as if it were about to ascend to the sky. This description suggests the size and majesty of the palace of the Koryŏ Dynasty (918-

In murals of old tombs from the Koguryŏ Kingdom, diverse colored patterns show the early appearance of *tanch'ŏng*.

1392), which existed around the 12th century. Sŏgung's book also included a description of the luxurious *tanch'ŏng* work, stating that "the handrail was painted in red and decorated with vine-flowers; the coloring was very strong, yet gorgeous, thereby making the palace stand out among other royal palaces."

Buildings from the Koryŏ Dynasty that remain standing today exhibit bright and soft coloring and the *tanch'ŏng* lining shows that the *tanch'ŏng* techniques

used during the Three Kingdoms period were further improved during the Koryŏ Dynasty.

During the Chosŏn Dynasty (1392-1910), Korean *tanch'ŏng* work was further developed and diversified. The general characteristics of *tanch'ŏng* during that period were a more expressive style and featured a complex unit pattern and decorative composition, along with more luxurious coloring.

There were a number of different types of *tanch'ŏng*; even in one particular building, patterns might be differentiated according to the part of the building they were located in. Nevertheless, *tanch'ŏng* patterns were systemized in a neat and consistent order. The system of patterns was categorized into four different types based on the structural characteristics and positions within the decorative composition. These four types included *moruch'o, pyŏlchihwa, pidanmuni,* and *tandok-muni.*

Moruch'o, also called *mŏrich'o,* was a pattern used in painting both ends of supporting beams (such as the ridge of a roof) or corners of a building (such as the tip of eaves). Although the pattern of *moruch'o* differed based on the time and the building, its basic patterns consisted of a green flower, water lily, pomegranate, bubble, and *whi* (feather), although it should be noted that the *whi* pattern was not featured in Koryŏ era *tanch'ŏng.* Using one sample pattern, *moruch'o* was repeatedly used in all the same parts of a building. Naturally, it occupied the largest amount of space and

he delicate and eautiful colors of anch'ŏng give it ajesty (left).

Tanch'ŏng of
Paekyangsa Temple.

was most noticeable. *Moruch'o* was therefore the basic *tanch'ŏng* pattern used in almost all types of buildings. During the 18th and 19th centuries, *moruch'o* developed quite diverse appearances, showing the vivid characteristics of Korean *tanch'ŏng* technique.

Pyŏlchihwa refers to decorative painting that expressed a storytelling technique and was placed in the gap between two *moruch'oes*. It differed based on the characteristics of the building, and was not used in palace construction; instead, it was most often employed in the construction of temples.

The content of *pyŏlchihwa* consisted of auspicious animals (such as dragons, horses, lions, and cranes), the *sagunja* ("the Four Gentlemen" or plum, orchid, chrysanthemum and bamboo), or scenes from Buddhist sutras. Though unrelated to the content of the sutras, the prevailing state of society of the time was also often depicted in temple *pyŏlchihwa*.

A *pidan* pattern refers to diverse coloring of rare and elegant designs or geometric patterns, and was used in various parts of the building, particularly in temples, while a *tandok* pattern involves the design of a single flower plant or animal, or the application of a single geometric or other pattern in one section.

The colors of *tanch'ong* reflected the characteristics of the period. During the Koryŏ period, parts of a building exposed to outside sunlight, such as pillars, were painted in red, while protruding corners of eaves

Colorful *tanch'ŏng*, where diverse and vivid colors intertwine.

Tanch'ŏng patterns were systemized into a set and consistent order. *Tanch'ŏng* of *Ch'ŏngŭi-jŏng* pavilion's ceiling.

or ceilings not exposed to sunlight were painted in greenish-blue, so as to enhance to the contrast of brightness and darkness. This application was known as the *sangnok hadan* (green-top, red-bottom) principle.

During the Chosŏn Dynasty, red, orange, blue, yellow, green, and *sŏkkanju* colors were used profusely. *Sŏkkanju*, also called *chut'o*, denotes red clay or ocher that yields a dark red or reddish brown pigment typically used for *tanch'ŏng* and pottery. This mineral pigment, basically ferric oxide of ferrous sulfate, is noted for its resistance to sunlight, air, water and heat. These were also mixed with white, Chinese ink color and others to derive various other colors. The colors were separated by insertion of white lines, thereby enhancing the distinctiveness of the pattern's outlining and coloring.

Ordinarily the order of colors used was determined by the characteristics, size, and appearance of the building. Usually, however, two to six colors were used following a set rule. For instance, when a gradual reduction of colors was desired from six colors, colors immediately after the first and immediately before the last colors were eliminated first to achieve a 5-4-3-2 order. Coordination of colors for *tanch'ŏng* consisted primarily of juxtaposing different and complementary colors. A technique of alternating a warm with a cold color was used to make the different colors more distinct from each other. Traditionally, typical pigments employed for *tanch'ŏng* were derived from *p'yŏnch'ŏng-sŏk*, a kind of copper ore, for dark blue and navy blue colors and from malachite for dark greenish blue. These pigments were preferred because of their vividness, durability and relative serenity. In addition, the vermilion pigment produced from clay, also a popular color for *tanch'ŏng*, was mostly imported from China's western regions and was hence highly valued.

The painting of *tanch'ŏng* was done by *tanch'ŏng-jangs*, artisans skilled in the work of tanch'ŏng. A *tanch'ŏngjang* artisan was referred to by a number of titles: *hwasa, hwagong, kach'iljang,* or *tanch'ŏng*. When the artisan was also a monk, he was referred to as a *kŭmŏ* or *hwasŭng*.

For palace construction, *tanch'ŏng* was done by a governmental office, *Sŏn-gonggam. Sŏn-gonggam* artisans exclusively carried out *tanch'ŏng* work for palaces and other places, such as guest houses and government buildings. Temples, on the other hand, had their own resident *tanch'ŏnjangs*. In addition to performing *tanch'ŏng* work , however, the temple artisans also engaged in production of other works, including Buddhist painting and sculpture. Although there were two different categories of *tanch'ŏngjang* for palace and temple painting , the technical procedures related to *tanch'ong* work were the same. The patterns and coloring systems were therefore identical for the two categories.

At the beginning of a project, a *p'yŏnsu*, or head artisan, was chosen by the initiating party of the construction project. The *p'yŏnsu* then selected the format of *tanch'ong* for the pertinent building and chose the patterns to be used. From mixing of colors to instruction of construction procedures, the *p'yŏnsu* was responsible for the completion of *tanch'ong* in its entirety.

Upon the beginning of *tanch'ŏng* work, a sample pattern was created for use in generating the same pattern of the pertinent parts of the building. This procedure was called *ch'ulch'o*. A bluish-green color was used as the base color, after which the pattern was placed on the desired spots of the building. This is done by pounding a powder sack over a paper transfer on which the design was outlined with pin holes. This work was referred to as *t'acho*.

After the above procedures, coloring could finally

Tanch'ŏngjangs are artisans skilled in the work of *tanch'ŏng*
The tradition still lives on through a handful of superb *Tanch'ŏngjangs*

be done. When coloring, each artisan painted only one color. The number of artisans employed in painting equalled the number of colors used in the design. Through such construction procedures, *tanch'ŏng* work was performed with efficiency in a systematic and regulated way.

Korea's *tanch'ŏng* developed in various different forms during 18th and 19th centuries. Shown here is *tanch'ŏng* on an old building.

In addition to its decorative function, tanchong was done for practical reasons as well. It was used to prolong the life of the building or equipment and conceal the crudeness of the quality of the material used.

Patterns

Patterns were devised by
people to decorate
their homes as well as
articles for daily use including
dress, furniture and various handi-
craft objects. Patterns are not only useful for ornament but symbolize human thought and philosophical and aesthetic pursuits. Patterns often have
their origins in early ideographs. They began as a
means to express basic needs and feelings about
one's surroundings and developed into a universal
form of decorative art.

Patterns

P atterns were devised by people to decorate their homes as well as articles for daily use including dress, furniture and various handicraft objects. Patterns are not only useful for ornamentation but symbolize human thought and philosophical and aesthetic pursuits.

Patterns often have their origins in early ideographs. They began as a means to express basic needs and feelings about one's surroundings and developed into a universal form of decorative art. Patterns can be largely divided into four main kinds based on motif-geometric patterns and patterns of plant, animal and nature motifs.

Geometric patterns consist of dots and lines forming symmetrical shapes in most cases. They include triangles, squares, diamonds, zigzags, latticeworks, frets, spirals, sawteeth, circles, ovals and concentric circles. It is interesting to note that most of these geometric patterns have their roots in primitive religious thought.

One example of a highly-developed decorative art
is the plant motifs on an old building.

One example is the fret design. The lightning pattern, which for primitive society depicted rain, represented their prayers for rainfall. A triangle symbolized reproduction and a woman's genitalia, and thus hope for childbirth. A swirl, resembling a whirlwind or a fern-brake, stood for death and the boundlessness of the universe.

Among favorite plant motifs were trees, flowers, fruits and grass. Animal designs engraved on stone or bone implements were related to the food-gathering activities of primitive humans such as hunting and fishing. Stone Age rock carvings feature various intriguing animal designs such as fish, whales, tigers, antlers and human figures. Nature motifs comprise landscapes, rocks, waves and clouds. Next, ritual implements, weapons and personal ornaments from the Bronze Age show more diverse patterns executed with advanced technique.

Paleolithic sites on the Korean Peninsula maintain some traces of early patterns. It is believed, however, that patterns began to be used on everyday objects during the Neolithic Age. The comb patterns on the Neolithic earthenware are among the earliest examples. Abstract delineation grew increasingly popular with time, so that most of the Bronze Age mirrors were engraved with fine lines that formed triangles, circles, concentric circles, radiation and star shapes.

More naturalistic patterns were employed in the Three Kingdoms period (57 B.C.-A.D. 668) and motifs inspired by animism appeared in the Koguryŏ Dynasty (37 B.C.-A.D. 668) as is evident in the tomb murals of the period. A typical example is that of the four guardian spirits–the blue dragon of the west, the white tiger of the east, the red peacock of the south and the black turtle-snake of the north. These four Taoist symbols of auspiciousness and authority appear over and over in all forms of Korean art.

Linear renderings of

metric and
al patterns
wo main
fs of Korean
tive art as
vn in a rock
ng in Koryŏng.

Comb patterns can be found in articles made for daily use during the Neolithic Age. Shown here is earthenware decorated in a comb pattern (right).

Since ancient times, Koreans have used various patterns to decorate different objects. The ten longevity symbols shown decorate a wall, from the late Chosŏn period.

Flower and
other motifs on
an old tile.

The *kwimyŏn*
one of the animal
patterns found on a tile,
Unified Shilla era.

Abstract delineations
in a mirror,
Bronze Age.

symmetrically arranged quasi-abstract phoenixes and dragons can be seen in many Shilla (57 B.C.-A.D. 935) ornaments. But trees, antlers and bird wings, evidence of Siberian shamanistic traditions, are central to the motifs found in the crowns and pottery of Shilla. The swirling cloud and flame motifs of Chinese origin decorate many personal ornaments and jewelry objects of Shilla aristocrats. Honeysuckles and lotus flowers adorn the crowns of the Paekche Kingdom (18 B.C.-A.D. 660).

A combination of Buddhist designs with shamanistic, Taoist and Confucian motifs is found in the arts of all periods. Lotus flowers, clouds, lightning and swastikas can be seen in nearly every Buddhist structure or painting, either singly or in various configurations.

Following the unification of the peninsula by Shilla,

Flower-patterned latticeworks, with rhythmical and symmetrical shapes, give a very harmonious look. Latticeworks are frequently found in temples.

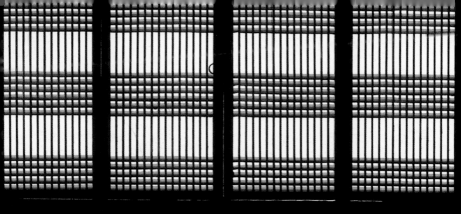

Wanja-patterned
latticeworks imbue
a sense of order.

allied with Tang China, in the seventh century, patterns grew more colorful and gorgeous with influences from China and Central Asia. Arabesques in the Tang style and Korean native style flower designs, called *posanghwa*, were obviously of more luxurious taste than the traditional honeysuckle and lotus patterns.

Delicate inlaid patterns on celadon, metalware and mother-of-pearl chests culminated the decorative art of the Koryŏ period (918-1392), which was characterized by a flowering Buddhist culture. Inlaying was a technique of carving out a desired pattern on the surface of a pierce of pottery or metal ware and filling in the recession with clay or gold or silver before coating the surface with glaze or lacquer. In particular, Koryŏ artists displayed adroit craftsmanship in bronzeware with silver inlay, which served as the foundation for the widely acclaimed inlaid celadon and mother-of-pearl articles in later years.

Naturalistic themes of leisurely, idealized life embellish many Koryŏ celadonware and lacquered articles. Line drawings of water fowl, willows, reeds, chrysanthemums, cranes and clouds attest to the refined poetic taste of the Koryŏ nobility. Other favorite motifs included the plum, orchid, and bamboo, which, together with the ubiquitous chrysanthemum, constituted the "four gentlemen plants" symbolizing the virtues of learned men of noble demeanor.

Many Koryŏ celadon vases, incense burners and *kundika* bottles were skillfully adorned with drawings of water birds floating on willow-lined streams, carefree urchins frolicking among lotus leaves and wild geese flying against the clear autumn sky.

With the advent of the Chosŏn Dynasty (1392-1910), which adopted Confucianism as the basic creed for state administration and public ethics, the Buddhist-influenced, subtle and tasteful Koryŏ-style decorative art gave way to relatively simpler styles reflecting the frugal lifestyle of a Confucian-dominated society. A preference for the simple and mono-chromatic is evident in the arts of this period.

The Chosŏn literati painting, characterized by simple but deft brushwork rendered in ink, finds a pleasant echo in the underglaze cobalt decoration of blue-and-white porcelain ware. Favorite motifs in both these genres included landscapes, flowers and birds, grapes, and the ever popular "four gentlemen" plants.

The coarse but charming *punch'ŏng* ware deserves attention as a significant transitional stage connecting the elegant Koryŏ celadon and the simple and

his celadon *maebyŏng*, plum vase, th an inlaid cloud d crane design is masterpiece of the ryŏ period. exemplifies the quisite and phisticated technique veloped during that riod of inlaying tterns taken mostly m nature, such as birds, wers and clouds.

The *t'aegŭk* is frequently seen in articles of daily use. Here the *t'aegŭk* pattern is found on a butterfly decorating a piece of furniture.

pragmatic Chosŏn porcelain. Coated with white slip and glaze, the utilitarian stoneware vessels are ornamented with carefree peony scrolls, fish with humorous expressions and stamped tiny chrysanthemum heads, among other motifs frequently used.

Despite an obvious predilection for monochromic simplicity, the wooden bracketing systems, pillars and beams of palace and temple structures provide rare examples of dazzling decoration with patterns of all imaginable motifs rendered in the five cardinal colors of red, blue, yellow, white and black. Dragon and phoenix motifs adorn the ceilings of the throne halls of palaces symbolizing the king's supreme authority.

The ten longevity symbols constituted a major theme of folk painting as well as the decorative motifs of handicraft objects used by people of all social classes. The ten objects, including rocks, mountains,

The *t'aegŭk* is the basic design motif of our national flag. Shown here is the reprinted edition (left and wood-block edition (right) used for printing the *t'aegŭk* (Korean national flag)

water, clouds, pine trees, turtles, deer, cranes, the fungus of immortality and the sun, made appealing motifs for folding screens, lacquered chests, ceramics and embroidery on clothes and other fabric items for daily use.

In the same Taoist strain of the world view, Chinese characters meaning longevity (*su*), happiness (*pok*),many sons (*ta nam*), and wealth and high social status (*pu kwi*), were widely used in stylized or pictorial forms. These characters embellish various articles of everyday use such as pillow pads, spoon cases and wooden wardrobes.

Attesting to the deep-rooted, Taoist-Confucian tradition among the Koreans is the frequent use of the *t'aeguk* pattern and the eight trigrams symbolizing possible situations and processes of the interaction between the two contrasting but mutually comple-menting elements of *yin* and *yang*.

The *t'aeguk* pattern, consisting of two whirling

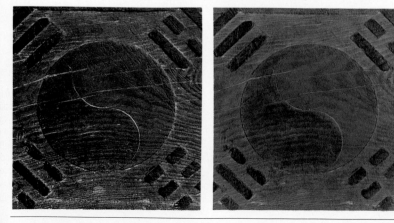

elements, symbolizes the "Great Ultimate," or the primary source of all reality. The two whirls stand for *yin* and *yang*, the cosmic elements of tranquility and activity, weakness and strength, dark and light, and male and female.

Chu Hsi, the chinese philosopher who founded Neo-Confucianism, said that the Great Ultimate is like the moon. It is one but its light is scattered upon rivers and lakes. Thus, he said, the Great Ultimate is both the sum total of all principles and principle in its oneness.

As seen in the Korean national flag, the pattern has *yang* in red at the top, and *yin* in blue at the bottom, symbolizing heaven and earth, respectively. Similar patterns of dualism are found on the doors of temples and shrines, clothes, furniture and daily objects such as fans and spoons.

Koreans march with *t'aegŭksŏn* fans in their hands during the 1988 Olympics, creating a beautiful wave of *t'aegŭk*.

A combination of Buddhist designs with shamanistic, Taoist and Confucian motifs is found in the arts of all periods. Lotus flowers, clouds, lighting and swastikas can be seen in nearly every Buddhist structure or painting.

Pottery

Korea boasts a virtually unexcelled cultural tradition of pottery. Deep-rooted in the nation's long history, Korean ceramics are world-renowned. In turn ceramics have greatly influenced the lifestyle of the Korean people. Pottery includes earthenware, ceramic ware, stoneware, and porcelain. Historical studies suggest that man first started making earthenware in approximately 10,000 to 6,000 B.C. The oldst kind of Korean earthenware found thus far dates back to 6,000 to 5,000 B.C.

Pottery

Korea boasts a virtually unexcelled cultural tradition of pottery. Deep-rooted in the nation's long history, Korean ceramics are world-renowned. In turn ceramics have greatly influenced the lifestyle of the Korean people.

Pottery includes earthenware, ceramic ware, stoneware, and porcelain. Historical studies suggest that man first started making earthenware in approximately 10,000 to 6,000 B.C. The oldest kind of Korean earthenware found thus far dates back to 6,000 to 5,000 B.C.

Korea's earliest earthenware was made by firing clay at a temperature of 600-800 degrees centigrade or sometime even 1,000 degrees centigrade. The oldest earthenware included those that were just dried without firing. This type of earthenware was only made for a certain period of time. Later on, as man's ingenuity increased, not only was the way of kneading clay improved, but kilns also began to be built that

This gourd-shaped vase, National Treasure No.116, is one of the most famous celadon pieces of the Koryŏ Dynasty.

Korea started using earthenware 7,000 to 8,000 years ago. A piece of earthenware from that time period.

could withstand the heat needed for firing.

Ceramics are produced by firing clay at a temperature ranging from 900 degrees centigrade to 1,000 degrees centigrade, which is then glazed. This process includes oxidization that turns the color of earthenware yellow, brown or red, and celadons and porcelains into yellow or brown.

Stoneware is fired in a kiln whose temperature exceeds 1,100 degrees centigrade. In this process, oxygen is limited to a minimum. Some stoneware is coated with either natural glaze or artificial glaze. This method of firing transforms the color of earthenware into grey, greyish and bluish-black, that of celadon into beautiful greenish-blue, and that of porcelain into mystic light blue. Porcelain is ceramic ware that is made of very pure white clay. It is shaped and glazed with feldspar before being fired at 1,300 degrees to 1,350 degrees centigrade. For that reason porcelain is translucent.

Koreans began to make porcelain in the Neolithic era (7,000-8,000 years ago). In the Three Kingdoms period (57 B.C.-A.D. 688), Koreans produced much more refined versions of earthenware that were fired at a very high temperature. Of exceptionally high quality were Shilla and Kaya earthenware that was fired at over

1,200 degrees centigrade. The surface of this earthenware is greyish-blue and is extremely sturdy, almost like iron.

With the beginning of the Unified Shilla era (668-935), the ground was laid for producing ceramic ware. Pottery soon took to making celadon in earnest and eventually some white porcelain. In the Koryŏ era (918-1392), the art of making celadon developed greatly, and celadon of extremely high quality was produced.

In addition to Koryŏ celadon, other kinds of pottery including iron-glazed and black-glazed pottery were also produced.

The unique, exquisite color of celadon, obtained

Earthenware found in
an old tomb from the Kaya Kingdom.

through an arcane method of firing with reduced oxygen, first appeared in the 11th century and was subsequently further refined. In the 12th century, pure celadon emerged as the most sophisticated Koryŏ celadon, and was used mainly by aristocratic households and Buddhist temples.

Koryŏ pottery reached its peak in the first half of the 12th century. During the reign of King Injong (r.1123-1146), the firing method further advanced to produce celadon whose almost mystic bluish or gray-green color, often described as 'kingfisher green,' defied comparison. The subsequent reign of King Ŭijong (1147-1170) saw remarkable advance in the technique of inlaying and drawing designs on celadons. In short, Koryŏ celadon is widely acclaimed as the best and finest type of pottery for its subdued yet clear, high-spirited bluish-green color, its graceful,

1

2

3

4

5

flowing curves, and its vivacious shape. Furthermore, Koryŏ celadon, with its poetic inlaid designs and especially its inlaid copper whose color is artfully transformed to look red, the first technique of its kind ever known in the world, represents the apex of the Koryŏ pottery.

The 13th century Mongol invasion of Korea brought a decline in Koryŏ pottery. As a result, the color, shape and decorative designs of celadon items changed. Celadon pieces took on a mostly dark greenish and opaque glaze and lost much of their graceful shape. Inlaid patterns became rough and were often omitted. Thus the quality to Korean pottery had climaxed with Koryŏ celadons as the Chosŏn era (1392-1910) began to unfold.

Chosŏn ceramics consisted of two major categories: a type of stoneware called *punch'ŏng* pottery and white porcelain. A product of the early period of the Chosŏn era, *punch'ŏng* pottery, made for wider use by the masses, is expressive of indigenous Korean folk art. During the period from the final years of the Koryŏ era to the early years of Chosŏn, celadon gave way to *punch'ŏng* pottery on which designs were inlaid, stamped, or painted with iron pigment, or scratched into the slip coating. The glaze on *punch'ŏng* pottery is light blue, and their shapes differ from celadon.

In the period from the late 13th century through the 15th century, Chosŏn white porcelain, a variation of celadon and Koryŏ white porcelain, was also produced. In addition, a new version of Chosŏn porcelain that was quite different from traditional Koryŏ pottery was produced. Thus, together with Koryŏ ceramics, *punch'ŏng* pottery and the new version of Chosŏn white porcelain, formed the mainstream of Korean pottery through the 16th century.

Punch'ŏng pottery is different in both shape and other characteristics from white porcelain. *Punch'ŏng* pottery varies greatly in its decorative designs, whereas white porcelain is made entirely of white clay and has no decorative designs on it. Overall, the color of Choso n pottery tended to be white.

The Japanese invasions of the Korean Peninsula in the late 16th century dealt a major blow to Korean pottery. During the invasions, numerous kilns were destroyed, and many Korean potters were taken as captives to Japan. All this caused a major setback to the development of Korean pottery, while these captured

Punch'ŏng pottery.

Punch'ŏng pottery
15th century,
National Treasure No.179.

White porcelain jar,
early Chosŏn era (mid 15th century),
National Treasure No. 219.

White celadon, early Chosŏn era.

White celadon pencil case.

Korean potters eventually gave a major boost to the rise of the ceramics industry in southern Japan. In particular, the devastation by the Japanese invaders virtually brought an end to the production of *punch'ong* ceramics, one of the two principal pottery styles of the Choson period.

From the first year (1392) of the reign of King T'aejo to the 27th year (1649) of the reign of King Injo of the Choson era, *punch'ong* and white porcelain constituted the main stream of Korean pottery, although *punch'ong* became increasingly dominant during the 15th century. However, beginning in the second half of the 16th century, the production of *puch'ong* pottery dwindled and virtually ceased before the 1592-1598 Japanese invasions took place. No *punch'ong* ware was produced after the Japanese invasions. *Punch'ong* basically resembles Koryo celadons in its form and shape. Yet, characteristically, *punch'ong* exhibits sprightly, daring and often humorous and yet gracious lines.

The shade of high-quality white porcelain produced in the earlier period of the Choson era is pale blue, reminiscent of the clear skies shortly after daybreak following a night of snowfall. The serene, dignified beauty of a white porcelain with no decorative design on it is virtually unrivalled.

This kind of white porcelain reached its heyday in the late period of the Choson Dynasty, although similar types of white porcelain appeared in

White porcelain peach-shaped ink container.

some quantities in the early period of the same dynasty.

During the reign of King Sejong (r.1418-1450), white porcelain with underglaze designs in cobalt blue was produced, though the quantity of such porcelain was relatively limited. Beginning in the second half of the 15th century, Korean potters produced white porcelain with underglaze designs in ferrous iron oxide. By the mid-17th century, the underglaze designs on such porcelains became more simplified and stylized,

White porcelain bottle, mid-Chosŏn Dynasty (17th century).

White porcelain jar, mid-Chosŏn Dynasty (early 18th century).

mostly depicting plants and flowers, such as chrysanthemums, as well as dragons. All these designs elicit the aesthetic beauty that is typically Korean.

This white porcelain underwent a major change in its shape and design during the middle period of the Chosŏn Dynasty, more specifically from 1651, the second year of King Hyojong's reign, to 1751, the 27th year of King Yŏngjo's reign—a period that followed the Japanese invasions of the Korean Peninsula (1592-1598) and the Chinese incursions into Chosŏn (1627 and 1636-1637).

White porcelain ware produced in that period became increasingly pure white in color and took on flat sides. The underglaze designs on the porcelain became less elaborate and more impressionistic in perfect harmony with both the color and shape of the porcelain. Much of the white porcelain, including flatsided jars, produced in the period was particularly noted for their luminous whiteness; hence they were known as 'snow-white porcelains.'

Some of the white porcelain also produced during this period is especially famous for their paintings of orchid designs emphasizing their unadorned beauty. In the middle to later period of the 15th century, there appeared white porcelain that exhibited the patterns of stylized paintings. These decorative patterns drawn on white porcelain became further simplified, accentuating their thematic expression in a unique manner.

In the period from 1752, the 28th year of the reign of King Yŏngjo, through the end of the 19th century, the final period of the Chosŏn Dynasty, even greater

White porcelain ink container, late 18th century.

variety of pottery was produced. However, as imperial Japan began to make increasingly overt attempts to occupy the Korean Peninsula in the late 19th century, a massive quantity of Japanese pottery products flooded the Korean market. Subsequently, the capital-rich Japanese set up large-scale pottery factories, causing the Korean pottery craft to decline rapidly.

Ceramic products mass-produced by the Japanese in Korea consisted mostly of artless porcelain pieces manufactured with machines, in sharp contrast with Korean ceramics that had been hand-made and

White porcelain dish, late Chosŏn Dynasty (late 18th century).

White porcelain jar (mid 19th century) (right).

fired in traditional kilns. Nevertheless, Korean potters continued to produce fairly large quantities of traditional jars, such as those used to store drinking water, soy sauce, and kimch'i, Korea's traditional pickled vegetable dish.

Today, Korean potters are making enormous efforts to recreate traditional pottery of highly artistic quality through kilns which have been rebuilt in the country side. The most notable kiln sites include Haenam-gun, Chŏllanam-do province, and Kwangju-gun and Ich'ŏn-gun, Kyŏnggi-do province.

Today, Korean potte make traditional jars used to store drinkin water, soy sauce, and kimch'i.

Recreating the pottery of their forefathers, Koreans continue to produce beautiful items.

Koryŏ celadon is widely acclaimed as the best and finest type of pottery for its subdued yet clear, high-spirited bluish-green color, its graceful, flowing curves, and its vivacious shape.

Changshin-gu
Personal Ornaments

The term *changshin-gu* refers to various objects worn for ornamental purposes. In Korea the original purpose of these ornaments was not only to enhance one's physical beauty but also to bring good luck and to chase away the bad. The ornaments were also symbols reflecting the social status of the wearer. The history of these objects dates back to ancient times. Tubular-shaped jade and necklaces made of animal bones were discovered among historical remains dating back to the Neolithic Age and numerous relics from the Three Kingdoms period (57 B.C.–A.D. 668) include exquisitely detailed ornaments made of gold, silver and gilt bronze.

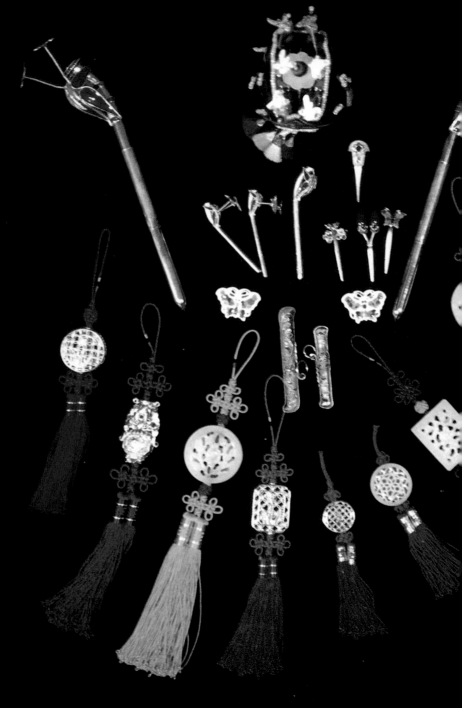

Changshin-gu
Personal Ornaments

The term *changshin-gu* refers to various objects worn for ornamental purposes. In Korea the original purpose of these ornaments was not only to enhance one's physical beauty but also to bring good luck and to chase away the bad. The ornaments were also symbols reflecting the social status of the wearer. The history of these objects dates back to ancient times.

Tubular-shaped jade and necklaces made of animal bones were discovered among historical remains dating back to the Neolithic Age, and numerous relics from the Three Kingdoms period(57 B.C-A.D 668) include exquisitely detailed ornaments made of gold, silver and gilt bronze.

The most representative Korean ornaments include headdresses and hair accessories, necklaces, earrings, chest pieces, bracelets, court hats, ring, and pendants. Primitive hairpins and combs made of animal bones are some of the hair ornaments that date from prehistoric times.

The history of personal ornaments in Korea dates back to ancient times. Shown are various traditional ornaments worn by women.

Hair ornaments from the third and fourth centuries were more delicate and splendid, and include combs, rod hairpins, and clasps used to hold hair together. Combs discovered inside the ancient tombs of the Shilla Dynasty (57 B.C. - A.D. 935) were all made of lacquered wood, and the teeth were fairly thin and long. A hair clasp discovered inside the tombs of King Munyŏng of Paekche resembles an elegant bird in flight with a head part followed by three long branches detailed to look like the billowing tails of a bird. Hairpins from the Koryŏ Dynasty (918-1392) are even more delicate and exquisite in their details, with a Chinese phoenix or rooster heads carved on the head parts.

Golden necklace, Shilla Dynasty.

Another object from the Koryŏ Dynasty is the topknot hairpin, which was used by men to hold their topknots in place. In addition to this practical purposes, it also served as an ornamental piece. Magnificent gold topknot hairpins from the Koryŏ Dynasty came in various shapes and sizes.

During the Chosŏn Dynasty (1392-1910) a national policy was declared imposing limits on the use of personal ornaments. Tight restraints on the use of gold and silver brought about a deterioration in the artistic value of the ornaments produced during this period

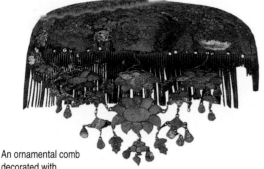

An ornamental comb decorated with golden flowers, Unified Shilla period.

and in the quality of craftsmanship in general. However, as a result, the production of ornaments using materials other than gold and silver flourished, and their use became widely popularized.

During the Chosŏn Dynasty, the use of rod hairpins was severely restricted, with social status dictating the use of different materials and shapes. Women of the royal court and high society wore rod pins made of gold, silver, pearls, jade, and coral, while those of lesser status were limited to ones made of wood, horn, nickel alloy, and brass.

The head shapes of the rod pins were also different according to social status. The queen and women of the royal court and high society wore pins shaped in the images of dragons and Chinese phoenixes, while

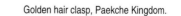

Golden hair clasp, Paekche Kingdom.

Rod hairpin,
Koryŏ Dynasty.

common folk were allowed only plain pins or those shaped like mushrooms. The head shapes and materials of the pins also varied according to the season.

Several new shapes of ceremonial hair decorations including the *ch'ŏpji* and *ttŏljam*, as well as hair picks and *taengki* (ribbons) emerged during the Chosŏn Dynasty. The *ch'ŏpji*, is a type of hairpin that women wore with ceremonial dress to enhance their beauty. It came in the shape of a phoenix or a frog. The phoenix-shaped pin was reserved for the queen's exclusive use, and the frog-shaped pin was for common folk. *Ttŏljam* was worn by women of high society on ceremonial occasions. It came in round, square, and butterfly shapes and a variety of other forms. The pieces were lavishly decorated with cloisonné, pearls, and other precious gems.

Magnificent topknot hairpins in various shapes and sizes (right).

Hair picks refer to all the ornamental pieces worn in chignons other than the rod pins. These include plain picks with pointed ends and practical ones that could be used as ear picks and also for parting one's hair. Chrysanthemums, lotus, apricot blossoms, and butterflies were some of the more popular shapes, and the picks were decorated with coral, jade, precious stones, cloisonné, and pearls. A *taengki* (hair ribbon) was a piece of gold-inlaid cloth that was used to hold a woman's hair in a braid. The ribbons came in a variety of

Ch'ŏpjis shaped like a phoenix (above) and a frog (below) worn by women in the royal court during the Choson Dynasty (right).

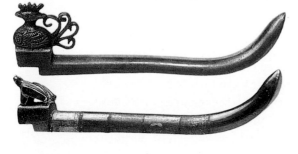

shapes and sizes. Along with these hair decorations, Koreans traditionally favored the use of earrings as ornamental pieces. The use of earrings also dates back to prehistoric ages, and they became more lavish and detailed with time. Earrings from the prehistoric ages included those made from animal bones or curved jade. Relics from ancient remains clearly indicate that even during this early period, Korean earrings came in a variety of shapes.

In particular, it is interesting to note that during the Three Kingdoms period (57 B.C. - A.D 668), earrings were popualr with both men and women. Earrings from this period can be divided into three groups according to their shapes: a

Ttŏljam lavishly decorated with cloisonne, pearls, and other precious gems, Chosŏn Dynasty.

single loop, a loop attached to the post, and those with multiple loops with lavish decorations dangling from one of them.

Materials used for earrings included gold, silver, and gilt bronze, with gold being the most popular. Among the relics of the Koryŏ Dynasty are pure gold earrings. Some are simple in design with three connected loops, while others are decorated with round beads. While the use of earrings wasn't as popular during the Chosŏn Dynasty, the period is noteworthy in that it brought about a revolutinary change in the way earrings were worn. Until then, earrings were worn by piercing a person's earlobes and inserting the posts but it was now possible to simply clasp them on the helices. Sometimes five-colored tassels were used to complement the simple ornamentation of the earrings.

Hair picks worn in chignons, Chosŏn Dynasty.

These types of earrings were reserved for ceremonial purposes and were not for everyday use.

The use of necklaces in Korea dates back to prehistoric times. During this period they were constructed from a variety of materials including animal teeth, bones, tubular jade, and jade stones. From the third to the seventh centuries, the use of necklaces grew more popular. The shapes became more diverse as well, and necklaces were worn as a single strand or in multiple (two, three, four, and six) strands. The more popular materials were gold and jade.

Chest ornaments are objects worn on the chest for decorative purposes and differ from necklaces according to their lengths. During prehistoric times, primitive chest ornaments were made by drilling holes into sea shells and connecting them with a piece of string.

Chest ornaments of the Shilla Dynasty became much more lavish and exquisite in detail. In particular, the chest ornament

A *taeng-ki* was a piece of gold-impressed cloth used to hold a woman's hair in a braid, Chosŏn Dynasty (left).
Gold decorated earring, Shilla Dynasty (right).

discovered inside the *Kŭmnyŏngch'ong* (Tomb of the Golden Bell) is spectacular in its beauty and is lavishly decorated with 152 glass beads. Another piece found inside a large tomb in Hwangnam is also exquisitely decorated with gold, silver, glass and jade.

Gold necklace (left) and a necklace, Shilla period, presumably from someone in high society (below).

One article of ornamentation that was widely popular throughout the history of Korea is the bracelet, whose use dates back to ancient times. Early bracelets were primitive, made from sea shells, but with time the use of a variety of materials such as bronze, jade, and glass became more widespread. Bracelets, along with earrings and rings were the most popular ornaments during the period of the Three Kingdoms. The discovery of numerous bracelets in relics from this period attests to this fact, and most of these were made from jade, glass and metal.

The finger ring was another popular piece of ornamentation throughout the history of Korea. As early as in prehistoric times, Koreans are known to have used rings for decorative purposes. A ring made from a piece of bronze plate was dug up from an ancient tomb dating back to prehistoric times, which testifies to its early use.

From the Shilla Dynasty, numerous silver rings

Necklace (above); gold and silver bracelets (below), Shilla Kingdom.

have been discovered, and the lavish and exquisite details on these pieces clearly attest to the high quality of craftsmanship of this period.

Representative rings of the Koryŏ Dynasty are a gold ring decorated with agate and another with green gemstones. Others include a pure gold ring with an embossed arabesque pattern, a silver ring with jagged design, a silver ring with exquisite engravings, and a plain copper ring without any ornamental design.

During the Chosŏn Dynasty, rings were the most popular ornaments along with pendants. The materials used to make these rings were also diverse; they include gold, silver, cloisonné, jade, agate, amber, green jade, pearl, and bronze.

Court hats and crowns were worn by the king and government officials. In addition to their ornamental purposes, they served to represent the wearer's social status. The higher a person's position, the more lavish the hat. During the Three

Kingdoms (Koguryŏ, Paekche and Shilla) period, each kingdom with its different social structure developed its unique style of court hat. Among those of Koguryŏ, the most outstanding is the gold court hat created in the image of a burning flame. This gold hat was constructed by attaching nine ornaments, each shaped to resemble a burning flame, on a gilt bronze plate. Two identical ornaments were then attached to either side of the hat for additional decoration. A gold court hat excavated in Hwasŏng-ni in Teadong-gun boasts a frontal ornamental piece resembling a half-moon.

Milhwa ring, Chosŏn Dynasty.

A gold court crown discovered in an ancient tomb in the Pannam area of Naju city dates back to the Paekche Kingdom. This crown is decorated with lavish ornaments on the broad front band and on each side. The most impressive crowns of Paekche are the ones discovered among the relics inside the tomb of King Munyŏng. The decorations on these crowns, presumed to have been worn by the king and queen, were cut from thin gold plates and created in the images of glowing haloes.

Among the most widely known crowns of Shilla is the one with five ornaments attached to a narrow band. Additional decorations on the three main ornaments on the front and on each of the sides resemble tiny twigs branching out of a tree, thereby creating cascading images of small mountains. During the Koryŏ Dynasty,

Gold court hats Shilla Kingdom (above right and Paekche (below right)

crown styles were deeply influenced by the Chinese: *Myŏryukwan* was a square, flat crown with dangling strings of small precious stones that was worn by the king with formal attire; *Wŏnyukwan* was a dark, silk hat with a jade ornament worn by the king when meeting his court; *Poktu* was a formal hat worn by those who had passed the highest civil service examination when receiving their appointments; and, *Samo* was a round, black silk hat worn by civil and military officials, and is donned these days by the groom in a traditional wedding ceremony. Court hats similar to those worn by the Chinese were still popular during the Chosŏn Dynasty. It was not until mid-Chosŏn that the *kat*, a uniquely Korean hat woven from horse-hair, emerged. Jade buttons and decorative egret shapes and strings were attached to the *kat* for ornamental purposes. Women's hats also grew more lavish as jewels were attached to flower hats and bridal tiaras, rendering them more appro-

Personal ornaments,
Chosŏn Dynasty
flower crown (left)
and pendant (right).

priate for special ceremonies.

The most representative item of personal ornamentation from the Chosŏn Dynasty is the pendant.

Pendants, worn by women on the outer bows or
inner bows of their blouses or on their skirts, were very
popular during this period. Materials included metals
such as gold, silver and bronze and gemstones such as
white jade, green jade, agate, red jade, blue stones, pure
jade, rough diamond, and malachite. The use of
precious stones and shells including amber, coral,
pearl, and tortoise shell was also common. The
pendants also came in a variety of designs with some
resembling animals such as bats, turtles, butterflies,
ducks, goldfish, cicadas, and terrapins while others
were shaped like plants including peppers, eggplants,
clusters of grapes, acorns, and walnuts. Often the
shapes were taken from objects that were part of
everyday life, and some pendants resemble bottles,
pouches, bells, gourds, drums, hourglass drums, and
spectacle cases.

Another personal item women carried was the

ornamental dagger. These were used for decorative purposes as well as for self-defense. The cylindrical dagger and others shaped like the letter "Z", squares, and octagons are only a few of the variety of shapes representative of this period.

Various ornamental daggers used for decoration and self-defense.

The most representative Korean ornaments include headdresses and hair accessories, necklaces, earrings, chest pieces, bracelets, court hats, rings, and pendants. Primitive hairpins and combs made of animal bones are some of the hair ornaments that date from prehistoric times.

Chasu
Embroidery

hasu, or embroidery, appears to have begun from the prehistoric era when the human race first started to make clothes. People used needles made out of bones of fish or animals to sew and weave animal skins and the bark or leaves of trees. Later, as civilization gradually developed, clothes began to be made, and with the advent of metal needles, embroidery emerged.

Chasu
Embroidery

Chasu, or embroidery, appears to have begun from the prehistoric era when the human race first started to make clothes. People used needles made out of bones of fish or animals to sew and weave animal skins and the bark or leaves of trees. Later, as civilization gradually developed, clothes began to be made, and with the advent of metal needles, embroidery emerged.

From then on, *chasu* has been developed as an art used to decorate textiles, and it, like other culture's embroidery, exhibits the nation's particular living environment, customs, and religion.

Korean *chasu* has a long history. As time changed, it has been a way of expressing Koreans' concepts of beauty. Along with weaving and sewing, *chasu* was a method of cultivating beauty in every corner of daily life. Sincere efforts went into every stitch and required delicate dexterity. Korean *chasu*, fully expressed the Korean character.

Korean embroidery fully expresses the Korean character.
Embroidery of the *Shipjangsaeng*, the 10 longevity symbols.

Among the Korean prehistoric excavated relics, a *pangch'u-ch'a* (a spindle cart) that was made out of earth or stone, big or small bone needles and stone needles, and needle pouches were found. Based on the finding of such weaving tools, it is clear that weaving and sewing existed during that period. Throughout the Bronze and Iron Ages, metal equipment for farming developed, thereby remarkably improving the farming industry. In Korea, *ma* (hemp) and *ppong* (mulberry) trees were cultivated; *myŏnp'o* (cotton cloth) and *map'o* (hemp cloth), as well as *hapsa* (twisted thread), were also produced. The development of weaving became the fundamental prerequisite for the development of *chasu*, and *chasu* was used to represent the status and rank of the ruling class in the form of decoraton on clothes, flags, or, wagons.

During the Three Kingdoms period, overall production technology developed greatly. Accordingly, weaving machines were improved and textile skills advanced; not only a variety of textile was produced, but also the quality was raised. Naturally *chasu* became popular. A trace of *chasu* that was embroidered with golden thread was found among the relics in the *Ch'ŏnma-ch'ong* (Tomb of the Heavenly Horse) in Kyŏngju, a good example that shows the status of *chasu* culture during that period.

During the Unified Shilla period, horse saddles and things related to everyday life, not to mention clothes, were decorated with *chasu*. Buddhist *chasu* was also commonly created. Particularly during the 9th year of King Hungdŏk (834 A.D.), a prohibition on clothing style was pronounced to strictly regulate the usage of textiles according to the *kolp'um* (aristocratic rank) system. During this period, due to the prosperity of Buddhism, much of the nobility eagerly gave donations for the construction or decoration of temples. As such a phenomenon accelerated, King Aejang prohibited construction of new temples and allowed only the repair of existing temples to be done to prevent the waste of materials. Usage of golden threads in Buddhist items was also prohibited. This indicates that high quality silk and *chasu* was used even in decorating objects in the *pŏptang*, the main halls of Buddhist temples.

Kongbangs (artisan shops) existed that were in charge of weaving, dyeing, and sewing. Artisans exported silk to China, and dyeing techniques were greatly improved at this time. Developments in dyeing techniques became a major factor that enabled the diversification and delicate coloring of textiles and threads.

In the Koryŏ Dynasty, *chasu* became excessively luxurious. *Chasu* of that era, for convenience sake, can be classified into *pokshik chasu, kiyong chasu, kamsang chasu,* and Buddhist *chasu.*

Pokshik chasu refers to *chasu* embroidered to decorate clothing. Dress was strictly regulated according to status and rank. For example, during the 3rd year of the reign of King Tŏkchong (1034), children and women were prohibited from wearing golden ornamental hairpins or embroidered silk clothes. During the 9th year of Chŏngjong's reign (1043), ordinary men and women were prohibited from decorating silk with dragon–or phoenix–patterns, along with golden stitches.

Also, during the 22nd year of King Injong's reign (1144), the King prohibited the use of golden thread in clothing and jade decoration in bowls. It can be inferred that during that era *pokshik chasu* was more than simply delicate and refined; it became excessively luxurious.

The queen and noble women of that time enjoyed red clothing with *chasu* decorations. The guardsmen who escorted the king largely wore silk clothes with flowers in five colors or bird patterns, and their belts were also often decorated with embroidered flowers in five colors.

Kiyong chasu embroidery decorated various materials used in the king's palace.

Kamsang chasu represented embroidery that had

The tradition of Koryŏ (918-1392) *kiyong chasu,* or the embroidery for the royal palace, is reflected in this folding screen decorated with the private seals of past kings.

been developed as a type of artistic piece. In other words, by use of *chasu*, various ornamental materials were decorated. Such *chasu* was prevalently used in folding screens in the bedroom or living room.

Buddhist *chasu* was embroidery related to Buddhism. During the Koryŏ Dynasty, Buddhism, as a means of defending the nation and promoting the prosperity of the dynasty, was supported as the national religion. As a result, more than in any other era, Buddhism was very prosperous; and *chasu* was heavily used in the statues of Buddha or various temples.

During the Choson Dynasty, marked changes occurred in many aspects of the country: political, economical, social, and cultural. Due to its early advocacy of an agriculture-first policy as its basic principle and the suppression of commercial industry, the handicraft industry did not develop. As a result, farmers concentrated on the production of food as their main occupation, and manual handicrafts became a secondary business. In spite of such circumstances, the production of clothing was prominently practiced.

Accordingly, the textile industry, related to production of clothing, as well as weaving and dyeing, generally became the responsibility of women. Female workers were encouraged to perform such work to increase productivity. It was also emphasized as a prerequisite virtue for any ordinary woman.

The legislation of the *hyungbae* (official insignia) system in the early Choson Dynasty was indeed noteworthy. Such a system which was related to the development of *chasu* required the systemization of government offices' manual work. The organization of the *kwan-ch'ong* (governmental offices) manual work increased from the Three Kingdoms era through the Koryo Dynasty. It peaked during the 15th century, which was the early part of the Choson Dynasty.

Hyungbae refers to the embroidered emblem that

A study of *hyungbae*, the embroidered emblems of official rank, is helpful in understanding the development of embroidery during the Choson Dynasty (1392-1910).

Hyungbae of cranes and tigers.

represented the rank of the government's civil and military officials. It was first implemented during the first year of King Tanjong's reign (1453). Later, after several modifications, the *hyungbae* system was improved and the emblems gradually became luxurious.

The embroidery on the king's state ceremonial dress symbolizes his high social status and authority.

As a type of a publicly-used embroidery, *hyungbae chasu* is good reference material in understanding the development of embroidery of that period. Artisans who were mobilized to produce textiles, and related items such as *hyungbae*, were among the most skilled people in the nation; they were placed in the central and regional governmental offices and devoted themselves to this field. They were responsible for the production of dresses and other textile products and embroidery decorations that were used by the royal family and high-ranking governmental officials.

Besides these organizations, there was an additional organization called the *subang* (embroidery room) that was exclusively responsible for embroidery works for clothes and miscellaneous materials for the family of the king. Upon completion of a certain level of education and expertise, women were selected to enter the palace to work in the *subang* and were registered; they exclusively produced *chasu* to meet the demands of the palace. During the Chosŏn Dynasty, interrelations among various artisan organizations and the *subang* provided the cornerstone of the palace *chasu*, which is also called *kungsu*. The *kungsu* tradition was sustained until the end of the Chosŏn Dynasty, and due to the standard format and the advanced skills of the artisans, the embroidery was delicate and perfectly executed.

In contrast with *kungsu*, there was *minsu* (folk embroidery) that was produced by the common people. Unlike *kungsu* that was specialized, *minsu* was a domestic skill passed down through the family or the region, and women in the household were in charge. As a result, in comparison with *kungsu* that was standardized, *minsu* reflected the characteristics of the individuals who created it. If Korean traditional *chasu* is classified according to function, it can be divided into pyŏngp'ung (folding screen) *chasu*, *pokshik chasu* decorating clothes and accessories, *chasu* used to decorate items used in the home, and Buddhist *chasu*.

Embroidered folding screens played an important role in the main events in life. For example, they were widely used at congratulatory banquets, such as those for anniversaries, birthdays–especially the 60th birthday–and engagements and for mourning ceremonies and other rites.

Embroidered folding screens were not only used in the various rooms of the home, but also in temples and shrines, as well as in the palace, depots, guest houses and lecture rooms.

The *pyŏngp'ung chasu*, therefore, exhibited great variety. The majority of screens, however, were of flowers and birds, the *shipjangsaeng*, or 10 longevity symbols, and *subok*, or Chinese characters for "long life" and "happines." For flower and bird screens, the peony, chrysanthemum, water lily, plum tree, and paulownia trees were matched with a couple of pheasants, a mandarin duck, phonixes, or ducks to symbolize a happy family. The *shipjangsaeng* are ten natural objects symbolizing long life: the sun, clouds, mountains, water, evergreen trees, bamboo, crane, deer, turtles, and the fungus of immortality.

There were many other embroidery designs, usually pertaining to lucky omens and education. Educational subjects, however, faded away from their original intention and later adhered to simple subjects. Hence, in *chasu*, emphasis was centered on creating beauty rather than on education. Embroidered screens, like painted screens, consisted mostly of eight panels, followed by 12, 10, 4 and 2 panels; there were even 20-

panel screens.

Pokshik chasu refers to embroidery on clothes and accessories. Particularly during the Chosŏn Dynasty, dress styles were highly differentiated according to class and rank, and patterns used in *chasu* follwed such distinctions. To represent high social status and authority, dresses worn in the palace usually had golden stitches or colored threads. *Chasu* was used in two styles: one was embroidering on the surface of the clothes directly, another was attaching *chasu* applique to the clothes. The first was used for the king's state ceremonial dress and various ceremonial dresses for the king's family members; the latter included miscellaneous dress embroidery, such as the embroidered patches on the breast and on the back of official uniforms.

On a *hwarot*, which was the ceremonial dress for the women in the palace, patterns of various flowers, such as peonies, chrysanthemums, fungus of immortality, and herbs, as well as various lucky omens and patterns of longevity were luxuriously embroidered. The clothing of males in the royal family and government officials did not have embroidery directy on the surface of the cloth; instead *hyungbae* decorated in patterns of cranes or tigers were attached to everyday clothing. *P'yojang,* an emblem which was attached to the dress of the king and queen, on the other hand, was differentiated from *hyungbae* and called *po*; its embroidery consisted of dragons or phoenixes.

For the most part, common people were not allowed to wear embroidered clothes, except for a *hwarot*, or ceremonial dress, at the time of their

1

2

3

4

5

wedding. Other materials that were embroidered included children's hats, vests, and belts. Especially, embroidered clothing for children used various colors and matching patterns to express their innocence.

Chasu also decorated numerous items used in the home. It would be impossible to list them all, but they include pillow cases, eyeglass cases, cushions and pouches for such thing as tobacco, spoons and chopsticks and brushes.

Unlike embroidery for purely decorative purposes, Buddhist *chasu*, which decorated temples and Buddhist statues, was created out of religious devotion. They were executed with extreme care by artisans of extraordinary expertise. Accordingly, there are many masterpieces which are preserved in temples and museums.

Everyday items:
. Pillow case
. Pouch
. Pouch for spoon
  and chopsticks
. Belt for *ham*
  (a bridal gift chest)
. Belt and pouch
  for a 1-year old baby

Korean chasu has a long history. As time changed, it has been a way of expressing Koreans' concepts of beauty. Along with weaving and sewing, chasu was a method of cultivating beauty in every corner of daily life.

Paper Crafts

Along with the indigenous and ingenious development of papermaking, Korea has established a deep-rooted tradition in the versatile use of paper. Among numerous traditional items of papercraft were such household goods as wardrobes, cabinets, chests, boxes, calligraphy desks, writing-brush holders, candlestands, room curtains, mats, cushions, comb holders and comb cabinets, trays, bowls with lids, basins, jars and food coverings.

Paper Crafts

Koreans have a centuries-old history of paper-making and have long enjoyed using indigenous good-quality paper.

Korea's oldest paper, called *maji*, was made from hemp. *Maji* is produced using roughly the following process:

Scraps of hemp or ramie cloth are soaked in water for some time and then shredded into tiny pieces. These pieces are ground in a grindstone to produce a slimy pulp, which then is steamed, cleansed with water, ground and placed in a tank. This raw material is pressed onto a frame and sun-dried while being bleached. This method of papermaking was most popular during the period of the Three Kingdoms (57 B.C.- A.D. 668).

In Paekche (37 B.C.- A.D. 660), one of the Three Kingdoms, paper thus made served as a chief medium for documenting historical events in the second half of the fourth century. Notably, Tamjing, a Korean

Korea's traditional paper craft lives on.

Buddhist monk and painter of Koguryŏ (37 B.C - A.D. 668), another of the Three Kingdoms, introduced techniques of papermaking to Japan in A.D. 610, the 21st year of Koguryŏ's King Yŏngyang. From all this, it is obvious that Korea had already developed an advanced method of papermaking by the early part of the seventh century.

In the Koryŏ era (918-1392), Koreans began to make paper from mulberries, or *taknamu*, which made it possible to produce paper in large quantities, and in the 11th century, Korea began exporting paper to China. Between the 23rd year (1145) of King Injong and the 18th year (1188) of King Myŏng-jong, mulberries were grown virtually all over the Korean Peninsula as the private paper manufacturing industry became a thriving business. The government encouraged paper-making by setting up a *chiso*, an administrative agency designed exclusively to promote the production of mulberry paper. Eventually, Koryŏ succeeded in producing fairly thick and sturdy paper whose obverse and reverse sides are both quite smooth and glossy. In later years, Korea's papermaking techniques further advanced, leading to the

A paper sewing box.

Colored paper was cut into the shape of a butterfly, a bat, a mandarin duck, the double-letter Chinese character meaning happiness, and a Chinese character meaning long life and to wish for good luck.

productin of *hanji*, a traditional Korean paper.

Along with the indigenous and ingenious development of papermaking, Korea has established a deep-rooted tradition in the versatile use of paper. Among numerous traditional items of papercraft were such household goods as wardrobes, cabinets, chests, boxes, calligraphy desks, writing-brush holders, candlestands, room curtains, mats, cushions, comb holders and comb cabinets, trays, bowls with lids, basins, jars and food coverings. Other popular papercrafts included tobacco pouches, spectacle cases, dippers, quivers, soldiers' armor, fans, umbrellas, apparel, footwear and hats, as well as artificial flowers, lanterns, and kites.

It is hard to tell exactly when Koreans began to

produce this plethora of items from paper, many of them for household use. However, historical documents indicate that the popular use of paper items dates as far back as the Three Kingdoms (57 B.C.-A.D. 668). This period left many books documenting important historical and other data. During that period, Korea introduced the method of papermaking to Japan and exported much-acclaimed Korean paper to China.

Interestingly, the great compilation known as the *Samguk yusa*, or "the Reminiscenes of the Three Kingdoms," notes that Koreans enjoyed making and flying kites made of paper, a clear indication that papercraft had already been developed to a considerable extent in Korea by that time.

In the early period of Chosŏn, under the reign of King T'aejo, a decree was proclaimed to emphasize austerity. Accordingly, artificial flowers made of paper replaced virtually all floral decorations at the sites of royal and private banquets and other functions from the beginning of the Chosŏn era. Artificial flowers most commonly used during the pre-Chosŏn period of Koryŏ were made of wax or silk cloth. During the reign of King Sejong (r.1418-1450), the use of paper flowers, in lieu of other kinds of artificial flowers, was further extended to Buddhist rites and festivals.

As the demand for paper increased rapidly, the royal court of King Sejong established a special office in charge of papermaking, leading to mass production of paper. During the early period of Chosŏn, the royal court supplied troops guarding the remote northern frontiers with *chigap*, armor made of specially treated paper. This armor was not only waterproof, but also effectively protected the soldiers from the severe cold during winter. More importantly, this armor was sturdy enough to serve as a protective covering against arrows, spears, swords, and other weapons. During the period of King Injo, *chigap* was steadily improved, often using scraps of paper and waste paper as raw materials. *Chigap* also inspired the invention of civilian

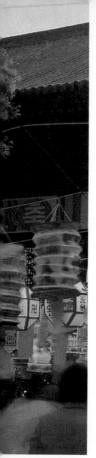

Paper flowers and paper lanterns first used in Buddhist rites and festivals during the reign of King Sejong are still used today.

attire made of treated paper.

Paper gained increasingly wider usage. For example, fans made of silk, widely used by Korean nobles, gave way to fans made of paper. In the middle period of Chosŏn, when tobacco began to be imported, tobacco pouches made of paper appeared and became the vogue. Other paper products made of old books and other used paper also made their debut. Frugality was considered a virtue in daily life. True to the spirit, Koreans came up with many other ways to make good use of scraps of paper. Paper reproduced from scraps of paper was used as lining for the walls of rooms. Scraps of paper were made into string that was durable enough to be used as a ring (in lieu of a door knob) attached to a door or as a clothesline.

Fans used by shamans.

A human cultural treasure makes various household goods by weaving paper cords.

In the early 18th century, Koreans began to produce cushions and mats made by weaving paper cords dyed in various colors. Subsequently, a variety of other household and personal items made of paper cords emerged.

According to Korean folklore, if one collects hair that falls out while combing one's hair and burns it outside the front door of one's home in the twilight of Lunar New Year's Day, it will ward off diseases and other evils. This folk custom made popular a bag made of oiled paper for keeping this hair. Also popular for the same reason was a comb cabinet.

In most cases, paper made from mulberry trees was used for traditional paper crafts. More specifically, second-hand mulberry paper—calligraphy-practice sheets, scraps left over from bookmaking or papering walls or the pages of old books—was especially favored. Traditional paper that was dyed various colors and oiled was also used.

Korea's traditional papercrafts can be divided into three major categories depending on the way the paper is used and on the shape of the items created. These categories are *chido kibŏp*, *chiho kibŏp* and *chisŭng kibŏp*.

In *chido kibŏp*, many sheets of paper are pasted together and then this multilayered, sturdy paper is shaped into a desired form. The products thus made ranged from tobacco pouches and workbaskets to needle cases and comb cabinets. Also in this category

A Korean mask, *T'al*, made with the *chido kibŏp* technique.

1. Chest, placed at the head of the bedding.
2. Shoe made of paper cord.
3. Oil lamp stand.
4. Comb holder.
5. Tray.

are paper products made by pasting many layers of paper on both the outside and inside of a pre-shaped bamboo or wooden frame. Products made through this technique included wardrobes and trunks.

Colored paper was used mainly for such products as wardrobes and trunks used by women. Favorite colors were blue, red, yellow, green and purple, all obtained from natural dyestuffs manufactured at home. Often, colored paper was cut into the shape of a butterfly, a bat, a mandarin duck, the double-letter Chinese character meaning happiness, and the Buddhist swastika and pasted onto paper products to wish for good luck.

Chiho kibŏp is the technique of using "paper clay" to make such kitchen items as bowls with lids and large scooped bowls. Paper clay is made from scraps of paper that are soaked in water and then crushed and mixed with an ample dose of glue.

Chisŭng kibŏp applies to the technique of making paper cords and weaving them into a broad range of household goods such as baskets, mesh bags, jars and trays. Other popular items made by weaving paper cords included stationery cases, mats, cushions and curtains. Still other paper cord products included quivers, dippers, powder-flasks, footwear, washbasins and chamber pots.

Some paper cord products including small calligraphy desks and trays were reinforced with wooden bars to withstand the weight of the goods placed on them. *Chisŭng kibŏp*, developed during the Chosŏn period, is a unique technique that enabled

A jewelry box (above).
A letter holder (right).

craftsmen to put otherwise useless scraps of paper to good use.

Most of these Korean paper products were properly varnished to enhance their appearance and durability while making them waterproof, since the use of lacquer for varnishing was rather discouraged under government regulations, the most commonly used varnish was *shich'il*, a mixture of unripened persimmon juice, rice glue and perilla oil. Colored papercrafts were often covered by liquified agar-agar and *pŏbyŏnyu*, a mixture of litharge, talc and alum which were boiled down in perilla oil.

All in all, Korean papercraft has long established itself as an ingenious part of the nation's creative and versatile folk culture.

Long-time papercraft collector, Ms. Kyung Kim shows various papercraft items.

Paper gained increasingly wider usage. For example, fans made of silk, widely used by Korean nobles gave way to fans made of paper.

Pojagi Wrapping Cloths

The word *pojagi* or *po* for short, refers to square hemmed cloths of various size, color, and design, which Koreans used to wrap, store, or carry things. *Pojagi* were not only practical and versatile items in the daily lives of Koreans, but were also very artistic. *Po* attests to the artfulness that Koreans seek even in the most mundane aspects of their everyday life.

Pojagi
Wrapping Cloths

The word *pojagi* or *po* for short, refers to square hemmed cloths of various size, color, and design, which Koreans used to wrap, store, or carry things. *Pojagi* were not only practical and versatile items in the daily lives of Koreans, but were also very artistic. *Po* attests to the artfulness that Koreans seek even in the most mundane aspects of their everyday life.

The use of *pojagi* in Koreans dates back to time immemorial, and historical records show the many ways in which they have been used. Although *pojagi* were created for everyday use, they also added flair and style to various ceremonies and rituals. During the Chosŏn Dynasty, the patterns and designs became particularly colorful. Because they are so easily folded and take up such little space, they could easily fit into, and become a colorful part of, everyday Korean customs and practices.

Pojagi were not only practical, but were also very artistic. *Chogakotpo* with triangular shapes.

Pojagi's place in Korean culture began in part with the folk religions of ancient times, when it was believed that keeping something wrapped was tantamount to keeping good fortune. A typical illustration would be the use of *pojagi* to wrap wedding gifts. Elaborate needlework is applied to such wrapping to wish the bride and groom much luck in their new life together.

Patchwork *pojagi* particularly reflects Korean artistic flair. *Pojagi* were born out of the habit of Korean housewives to make good use of small, otherwise useless pieces of leftover cloth by patching them up into useful wrappers. As time went by, the patchwork itself became a highly creative and artistic craft.

Embroidery of various figures and characters also adds to the beauty of *pojagi*. The handicraft can often reach the beauty of levels of artistic accomplishment. Embroidered *pojagi* are known as *supo*, the prefix *su* meaning "embroidery."

A popular motif on *supo* are trees, which to Koreans have represented the most sacred of living things. Since ancient times, Koreans have worshipped trees as the physical embodiment of sacred spirits and miracles. The trees on *supo*, therefore, bespeak of the prayers of their creators for good fortune.

Other favorite motifs for *supo*, include flowers, fruits, mandarin ducks and other symbols of goodness, which reflected the Korean well-wishing that goes into the making of *pojagi*. Each symbol represented something; for example, pomegranate stood for many births and many sons. The basic colors of *supo* are blue, red, yellow, white, and black, the fundamental colors of nature as postulated in the *yin-yang*, theory of five

Pojagi embodies the Korean artistic flair. *Chogakpo* with triangular shape (above), traditional *pojagi* with flower motif (middle), and rainbow-striped *po* (below).

primary elements (metal, wood, water, fire, and earth), which was an important element in the way Koreans understood the workings of the universe. *Pojagi* have thus been closely related to the everyday beliefs and practices of Koreans. They are convenient and safe carriers and protectors. As such, they perform the same functions as the western bags, but are far more versatile. Bags and luggage generally have standard sizes, but there was no standard size for *pojagi*. It would be difficult to find a western bags that can fit a watermelon without the loss of much space; however, a *pojagi* will do the job spendidly.

Koreans have farming origins, and in the quiet, peaceful existence of their agricultural communities, they have always had a tendency to find playfulness and beauty in the most mundane things in life. The colorful *pojagi* culture is one result of their inclination to combine the practical and the pleasing. As the centuries went by, the craftsmanship became even more elaborate and diverse, and *pojagi* came to embody the artistic sensibilities of everyday Koreans.

The many uses of *pojagi* can be categorized

Chogakpo is notable for its elegant design. *Moshi chogakpo* (above) and *chogakpo* made with colorful patches of cloths (below).

Koreans still use *pojagi* made with leftover cloth.

as follows:

1. *"Sang-yongpo"* (daily use *po*):

"Chondaepo" (money belt *po*) to wrap things (such as money) in and tie around the waste or shoulder;

"Pobusangpo" (backpack merchant *po*) used by petty merchants to carry their goods;

"Sangpo" (table *po*) to cover table with;

"Iblulpo" (blanket *po*) to wrap blanket in;

"Ppallaepo" (laundry *po*) to wrap laundry items in;

"Posŏnpo" (socks *po*) to keep socks in;

"Ch'aekpo" (book *po*) to keep and carry books in;

"Hwoetdaepo" (hanger *po*) to cover clothes racks with;

"Kanch'alpo" (letter *po*) to keep letters and documents in;

"Kyŏngdaepo" (dresser *po*) to cover a dressing stand with.

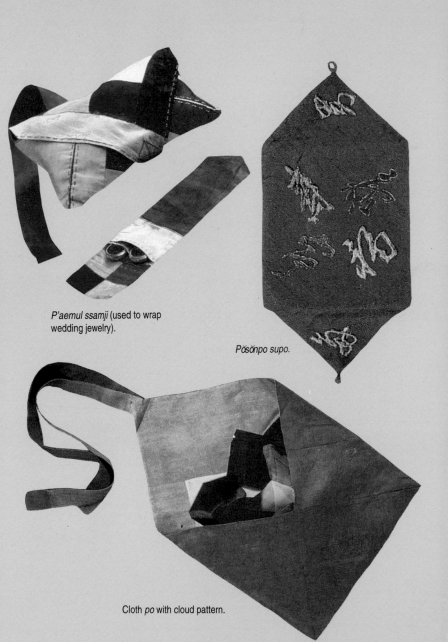

P'aemul ssamji (used to wrap wedding jewelry).

Pŏsŏnpo supo.

Cloth *po* with cloud pattern.

A popular motif
on *supo* are trees.
*Yŏnhwamun ham
patch'impo*
(a gift chest was
placed here).

Supo with flower motif.

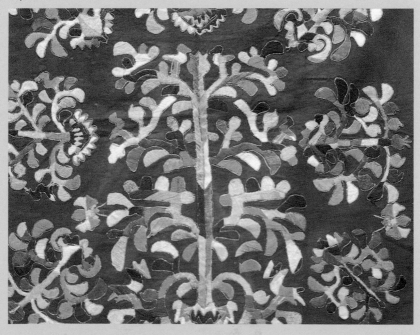

Colorful cloth *po* with patterns seen in a modern abstract painting.

2. *"Hollyeyongpo"* (wedding *po*):

"Hampo" (gift chest *po*) to wrap the "ham" in;

"Kirŏkipo" (wild geese *po*) to wrap the ceremonial pair of wild geese in;

"Yedanpo" (ceremonial present *po*) to wrap the gifts from the bride's family to the members of the groom's;

"P'yebaekpo" (bowing *po*) used when the new couple offers ceremonial bows to the members of the husband's family.

3. *Pojagi* used in Buddhist rites:

"Majipo" used to wrap the food offered to Buddha;

"Kong-yangpo" used when providing elders with food;

"Kyŏngjŏnpo" (scripture *po*) used to keep scriptures in.

4. *Pojagi* for special uses:

"Myŏngjŏngpo" used to cover the official recording

of the deeds of the deceased during a funeral;

"*Yŏngjong bong-anpo*" (portrait enshrining *po*) used when enshrining the portrait of a deceased;

"*Kiujepo*" (prayer-for-rain rite *po*) used when praying to heaven for rain;

"*Chegipo*" (ceremonial dish *po*) used to keep the dishes used during rites.

Pojagi can also be categorized according to their make-up, color, material, and design as well as the different classes of people who used them.

1. Different users:

"*Minpo*" (folk *po*) used by common people.

"*Kungpo*" (palace *po*) used within the confines of the royal palaces.

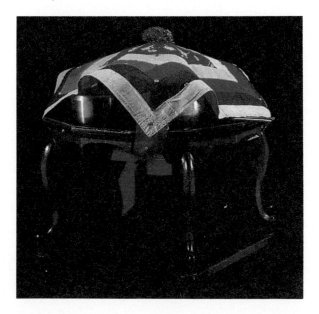

Sangpo.
Pojagi are ubiquitous and indispensable in the lives of Koreans.

2. Make-up:

"Hotpo" (single layer *po*) made of a single sheet of cloth without inner lining;

"Kyŏppo" (double layer *po*) made with inner and outer sheets;

"Sompo" (cotton *po*) made with cotton inner lining;

"Chogakpo" (pieces *po*) made by sewing small pieces of cloth together;

"Shikjipo" (oil paper *po*) made partially or entirely of oiled paper;

"Nubipo" (quilted *po*) made by quilting the materials.

3. Color.

"Ch'ŏngpo," (blue), *"Hongpo"* (red), *"Ch'ŏnghong-po"* (blue-red), *"Osaekpo"* (five colors), *"Ach'ŏngpo"* (dark blue), etc. depending on the color.

Chogak sangpo.
Pojagi are a very familiar part of everyday life.

4. Material:

"Sapo" (silk *po*) made of light and thin silk;

"Myŏngjupo" made of particularly fine silk;

"Hangnapo" made of silk gauze;

"Moshipo" made of ramie fabric.

5. Design:

"Hwamunpo," or flower figure *po*;

"Sumokmunpo," or plant-and-tree figure *po*;

"Yongmunpo," or dragon figure *po*;

"Unmunpo," or cloud figure *po*.

In all of their diverse manifestations, *pojagi* have been ubiquitous and indispensable in the daily lives of Koreans. When a daughter was married off, the parents made sure that she took with her dozens of *pojagi* made with the utmost care and well-wishes. Through her and the generations of Korean women that went before and after her, the *pojagi* culture has flourished in Korea.

Korean *pojagi* continue to flourish with their versatility and myriad designs. *Myŏngju chogakotpo.*

Pojagies are convenient and safe carriers and protectors. As such, they perform the same functions as western bags, but are far more versatile.

Peace be with you.

Hae Geum kang
Soo Hong Park.

April 11, 2004